Borders

& Finishing Touches 2

Bonnie K. Browning

American Quilter's Society

P. O. Box 3290 • Paducah, KY 42002-3290
FAX 270-898-1173 *www.americanquilter.com*

Located in Paducah, Kentucky, the American Quilter's Society (AQS) is dedicated to promoting the accomplishments of today's quilters. Through its publications and events, AQS strives to honor today's quiltmakers and their work and to inspire future creativity and innovation in quiltmaking.

Editor: Barbara Smith
Graphic Design: Lynda Smith
Cover Design: Michael Buckingham
Photography: Charles R. Lynch, Bonnie K. Browning
Published by American Quilter's Society

Library of Congress Cataloging-in-Publication Data
Browning, Bonnie K., 1944-
    Borders & finishing touches 2 / by Bonnie K. Browning.
      p. cm.
    Summary: "Step-by-step techniques for adding borders to quilts by hand or machine stitching. Technique for making folded paper templates. Border details for swag, piping, scallops, prairie points, and shark's teeth"--Provided by publisher.

Includes bibliographical references and index.
ISBN 1-57432-891-3 (alk. paper)
1. Patchwork. 2. Quilting. 3. Borders, Ornamental (Decorative arts) I. Title: Borders and finishing touches two. II. Title.

TT835.B736 2005
746.46--dc22
                    2005031768

Additional copies of this book may be ordered from the American Quilter's Society,
PO Box 3290, Paducah, KY 42002-3290;
Toll Free: 800-626-5420, or online at
www.AmericanQuilter.com.

Dedication

To the many students who have taken my classes over the last twenty years: It is because of you that I keep stretching and learning. May you all make beautiful borders to fit your quilts.

To my husband, Wayne, who is always there: We are still enjoying the journey that quilting is taking us on.

To my mother, Mary Kirkland, who continues to inspire me: May I live to be 80 plus years young and have half your energy.

Acknowledgments

Special thanks to these special quiltmakers who so willingly shared their quilts and techniques for this book:

Lois Embree Arnold, Montgomery, Alabama
Klaudeen Hansen, Sun Prairie, Wisconsin
Klonda Holt, Kansas City, Missouri
Deb Karasik, San Francisco, California
Judy Laquidara, Owensboro, Kentucky
Janet Mednick, San Francisco, California
Gladi Porsche, Lee, New Hampshire
Linda M. Roy, Farragut, Tennessee
Linda Scholten, Oxford, Ohio
A. B. Silver, Carlsbad, California
Lynda Smith, Paducah, Kentucky
Susan Stewart, Pittsburg, Kansas
Helen Umstead, Milford, Pennsylvania

To these companies who have provided products:
    Bernina of America, 200E Bernina sewing machine
    Clover Needlecrafts, Inc., fabric markers, quilting notions
    Hobbs Bonded Fibers, cotton batting
    Starr Designs, hand-dyed fabric

To Meredith Schroeder and all the staff at the American Quilter's Society, for adding all the finishing touches to make my books better.

Contents

Introduction

In 1997, I authored my first book on borders, *Borders & Finishing Touches* (AQS). Since that time, we quilters have created more beautiful borders on our quilts and added a variety of new finishing touches, too. I hope you will use this book as a good resource when you are looking for border ideas or for the how-to for a special finishing technique.

You will find an expanded Border Primer, with basic information on borders and how to get them to fit the edges of your quilts. In teaching my border class, I have found that the technique of folding adding-machine tape to be a method that is something anyone can do, because you don't need to use a ruler or math to make your borders and special edge treatments fit perfectly for any size of quilt. Whether you want borders that are plain, pieced, or appliquéd, you can make them fit.

Someone once told me that you shouldn't do mitered borders because you could only make a few good ones in your lifetime. Don't let that be your mantra. Mitered borders can be sewn successfully if you mark them correctly, and I share my tips for doing that on page 18.

The Finishing Touches section includes a variety of techniques on binding, piping, prairie points, rickrack insertion, shell-scalloped edges, dogtooth, and shark's teeth techniques. Have you tried making prairie points with piped edges?

In the pattern section, there are patterns for using a simple technique like a shaped border with piping in MERDIE'S POPPIES; a beautiful quilted feather border in THE GLISTENING ROSE QUILT by Judy Laquidara; the peek-a-boo appliqué technique used by Linda M. Roy in her Best of Show winning quilt SPICE OF LIFE; the complete pattern for the WINDMILL – TWISTED LOG CABIN quilt shown in the opening of the *Simply Quilts* television show; or the exquisite appliquéd border on KEEPING AUTUMN WITH ME by Gladi Porsche, and much more.

Be sure to read "Bind for Glory" by A. B. Silver, on page 51. The moral of this story is that every book gives you a variety of techniques to try. Some will work for you and some won't. I hope that the methods I've provided will help you make borders that fit your quilts and give you some finishing touches to make your quilts extra special. Try them—they may be just the thing to make your next quilt a prizewinner!

Always in Stitches,

Bonnie Browning

Bonnie K. Browning

The Border Primer

Does every quilt need a border? The answer to that question is "no." To border or not to border your quilt is one of the design decisions you must make. A border can be added for several reasons:

- to enhance the center of the quilt
- to define a section or the whole quilt
- to provide a frame
- to bring out the colors in the design
- to stop the design in the center
- to enlarge the size of the quilt

The color of the border plays an important role. A dark border has the effect of lightening and enlarging the quilt center, while a light frame serves to darken and shrink the image.

The designs in your borders can contain formal geometric lines or free-flowing, spontaneous shapes (vines, flowers, etc.). Between these two extremes, there are infinite gradations from relaxed to formal designs. The design is your own decision. You can take what you have learned from history or from nature, or just use your own experience and just do it! The results make your quilts your very own.

Experiment! Explore! Add excitement to your quilts with borders!

Making Borders Fit

Before beginning any borders, you need to know how to make a border that will accurately fit the quilt top. Begin by checking the top and bottom edges with the center of the quilt to determine if the edges and the center are the same. You can do this all in one step by folding the top and bottom edges to meet in the center of the quilt. Judges will often use this technique to take a quilt measurement to see how uniform your quilt is. *Photo 1–1*

If these three measurements are not the same, check the seam allowance used in assembling the quilt top (the seams in the blocks, the sashing seams, or the seams between blocks). If the difference is ½" or less, average the three measurements together and make the border that length. You can easily fudge up to ½" as you fit the borders to the edges of the quilt, either by stretching or gathering the fabric slightly. You will also need to compare the sides and down the center of the quilt to determine the length of the side borders.

If the difference is more than ½" it is best to stop and find out why. Measure the blocks. Are they the same size? Are the sashing strips the same width? Fix any blocks that need to be restitched to make them the correct size. It can also be something as simple as a sashing that was cut the wrong dimension. Fix it now, before you sew on the borders.

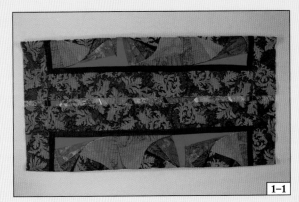

Fold top and bottom edges to meet in the center.

Helpline

Width of Borders

To help keep the width of the border in scale, try using a dimension from the blocks used in the quilt; that is, use a 2", 3", 4", or 6" border if 12" blocks are used.

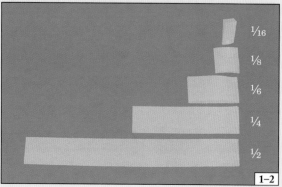

Border divisions

Adding-machine tape cut finished width (minus seam allowances)

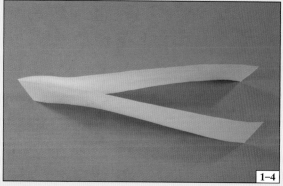

Folding paper in half

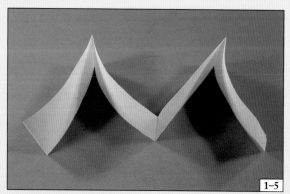

Folding paper in fourths

Many times, we want to divide the edge of a quilt into equal segments to make a specific type of border. Here are some examples of border divisions and possible designs. *Photo 1–2*

½ = Divide the border in half for a two-segment border, such as an appliqué that mirrors from side to side, or simply use two diagonally-split rectangles to frame the center.
¼ = swags
⅙ = undulating vine
⅛ = large pieced blocks
1⁄16 = small pieced blocks or scallops
1⁄32 = sawteeth, shark's teeth, dogteeth, prairie points

Folded-Paper Template
Follow these step-by-step paper-folding instructions to make an accurate template to divide any size of border accurately—all without using a ruler. A roll of adding machine tape is easy to handle for this purpose.

The width of the adding-machine tape has nothing to do with dividing your quilt edge equally.

You could be using freezer paper or any other kind of paper that can be cut the length of your quilt edge. I use adding-machine tape because it is inexpensive and is easy to work with. If you mess it up, just cut a new strip and start over.

Read these three rules before you begin making a paper template for your border:

Rule 1: All dimensions used for dividing a border are for the finished size of the quilt edge. Always use the finished size when determining divisions of the edge of your quilt. Seam allowances will be added to the individual elements (pieced blocks, squares, rectangles, scallops, etc.) when you are ready to work in fabric.

Rule 2: Ignore the corner until you have decided on the style of your border.

Rule 3: Read Rule 1 again! Fold your paper template for the finished size then add your seam allowances before cutting your fabric.

1 Check the accuracy of your quilt edges by folding both edges to the center. Cut a strip of adding machine tape the exact length of this edge. If you look at the edge of your quilt, you have seam allowances on

both ends of that quilt, correct? What was Rule 1? We need the finished length of that edge. So, let's subtract ½" from your adding machine tape to give you the finished edge of the quilt. *Photo 1–3*

2 Now, let's begin to fold the paper. First, fold the paper in half, meeting the two ends, and make a sharp crease in the paper. *Photo 1–4*

3 Let's fold the paper again: Pick up one end of the paper and place it inside the first fold. Crease the paper. Always fold only one layer of paper at a time. So, to complete dividing the paper into fourths, pick up the other end and place it inside the first fold. You will find there is less distortion if you fold accordion style rather than continuing to fold the paper over on itself. You have now divided the edge of your quilt into four equal pieces. These four equally divided spaces would be good for making a swag border. *Photo 1–5*

4 If you want to make smaller units, such as pieced blocks for the edge of your quilt, pick up the end of the paper and meet it to the nearest fold. Take that fold and meet the next fold, continuing until you have folded the entire strip. Occasionally, you will need to change an "outie" fold to an "innie" so the folds will nest inside one another. *Photo 1–6*

Once you have folded the entire strip into sections, measure one segment of your strip. The measurement is from one fold to the next. This is the finished size each of your pieced blocks will need to be. Please note that the only time you have to use a ruler in this technique is to measure from one fold to the next to determine the size of your finished block. **If the dimension is a segment smaller than the lines on your ruler, use the next line on your ruler, making the blocks slightly larger. To make the border fit properly, you may need to take a scant larger seam allowance when joining the blocks to account for the extra amount you added.** *Photo 1–7*

To make a pattern for your pieced block, remember that this measurement is the finished size of the block. You will need to draw your block and add seam allowances for each part of the pieced block.

For rectangular quilts, you will need to make a paper strip for the sides of the quilt and another strip for the top and bottom. Occasionally, you will need to fold one edge (say, the sides of the quilt) into even segments (2, 4, 6, 8). To get a uniform size for the other edge (the top and bottom), you may need to fold the paper into thirds first and then into even segments. Make the fold into thirds by sliding the paper back and forth until the segments are even. *Photos 1–8 & 1–9*

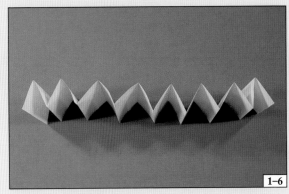

1–6

Paper completely folded

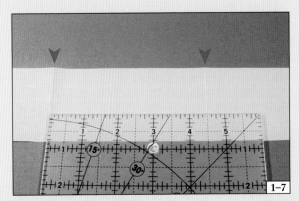

1–7

Measuring from fold to fold

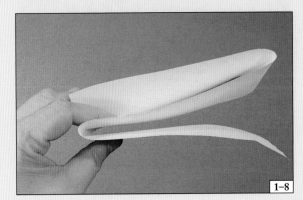

1–8

Folding paper in thirds

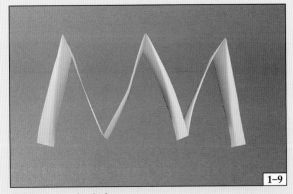

1–9

Folding paper in sixths

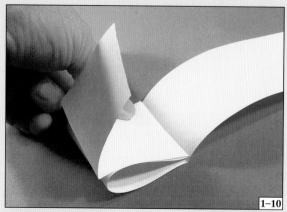
Folding into first fold

PLEASE, NO MORE PINKED SAMPLES!
Linda Scholten, Oxford, Ohio

Helpline

Butted Border Calculator

Top and bottom borders = finished width of the quilt.

Side borders = finished length of quilt + 2x finished width of border + ½" for seam allowances

Then you can start at the end of the paper and fold it into the first fold and crease the paper. Pick up the fold and meet it to the next fold. *Photo 1–10*

If you have a very large quilt, you can make your paper equal to half the finished length of the quilt edge. This will be easier to handle. Just don't forget that you will need to cut the fabric borders twice the length of your paper template for a plain border, or you will need twice as many pieced blocks for a patchwork border.

If you decide to create a special design in the corners of your quilt, use the finished size of the corner to develop the corner design. Add seam allowances. See page 16 for a corner treatment idea.

Border Designs

A quilt does not have to have a border, but if you decide it needs one, you will want to choose a design that enhances the center of the quilt. Sometimes, a simple border is enough. Other times, a more complicated border may be the piece de resistance.

No Border

Log Cabin quilts often do not have borders. Quilts that are set on point with alternating plain blocks and one-patch blocks are good examples of typically borderless quilts. Blocks that create an irregular edge, such as Grandmother's Flower Garden or Double Wedding Ring are also often made without borders.

Changing Color and Value

The color scheme of the blocks can be changed to simulate a border. You can simply change the value of parts of the blocks on the edges to create a border-like design. Remember to adapt the corner blocks as well.

In her quilt PLEASE, NO MORE PINKED SAMPLES! Linda Scholten used navy triangles to complete the diagonal setting of her quilt and also created a faux border by the change in color from the rest of the quilt. This is a very successful method to use when the blocks are set on point. There is no need to add another border unless you want to make the quilt larger. *Photo 1–11*

Single Bands

A single-band border can help frame or contain the motion of the central part (body) of the quilt, and it can finish a busy quilt without overpowering the central design. This is the simplest border that can be added. All you need to decide is the border width.

For MIZ SUKEY DIVINE, a quilt inspired by poet Sukey Divine, the author added another detail to simulate photo album corners by making a faced V-shape that was stitched to the corners of the quilt before the single-band border was added. Do you remember the 1950s with pink diners, ragtops, lots of beads, and crinoline underskirts? *Photo 1–12*

MIZ SUKEY DIVINE, by the author

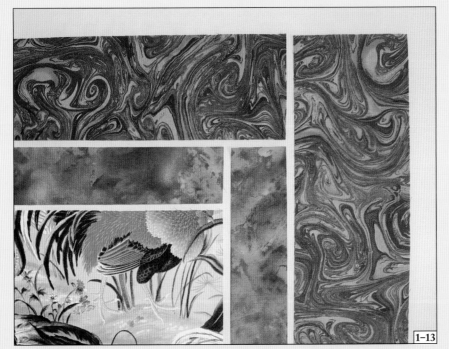

Add butted borders one at a time.

Butted Bands

For borders with butted corners, cut the top and bottom borders as long as the quilt body is wide. The side borders are cut the length of the quilt plus twice the finished width of the border plus ½" for seam allowances. (You can sew either the top and bottom or the side borders onto your quilt first, but for a large quilt where the side of the bed is visible as you enter the room, start with the top and bottom so the side borders will be one continuous strip without seams.) It is always a good idea to remeasure after you've added the first set of top and bottom borders before you cut the side borders. For multiple butted borders, sew all four sides of border 1 to the quilt, remeasure for the next border, add it to the quilt, and so on. *Photo 1–13*

FREEDOM, by the author

Multiple Bands

Borders made of multiple bands can add another design element and provide a more substantial frame to a quilt. To determine the size of the bands, use a dimension of the blocks; that is, if 15" blocks are used in the quilt, 3" (⅕ of the block), 5" (⅓), 7½" (½), or 10" (⅔) borders would appear in scale with the rest of the quilt top. If three bands are used together, they could be 3", 7½", 3"; or 3", 5", and 10" could be used if a wider border is desired.

Multiple bands can be cut individually and added to the quilt one at a time, or they can be added as a unit for mitered borders. If you stitch them together, calculate the length of each border carefully, using the border-cutting formula for mitered corners (see page 21). *Photo 1–14*

Geometric Designs

When geometric ornaments are used in the border, try selecting elements that are used in the blocks to help continue the design from the center to the edges of the quilt. For example, for pieced blocks with triangles, use some of the same triangles in the border. The triangles could be resized, made smaller or larger, but the design element would be the same. This same technique can be used for other pieced design elements.

Squares

Simple alternating squares in two or more colors can make an effective border. Multiple rows of squares make a checkerboard border. A border with squares looks attractive with a single-band border on either side. If you use one color on one side and a second color on the other side of the squares, you create a tooth-like border.

Klaudeen Hansen used simple squares in many colors to create the inner pieced border in this GRANDMOTHER'S CHOICE quilt. Notice how she used a single square on the long sides to join the outer border pieces together rather than splicing the plain border strips together. *Photo 1–15*

GRANDMOTHER'S CHOICE by Klaudeen Hansen, Sun Prairie, Wisconsin. Quilted by Irene Reising.

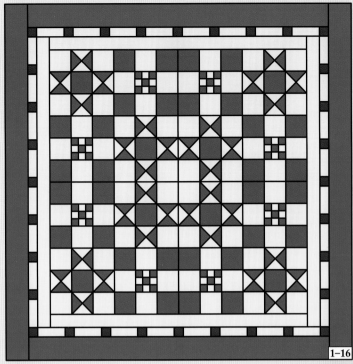

Border sample of squares and rectangles

Spaced Squares

Squares alternating with rectangles can add more variety than using only squares. Sometimes breaking up the squares with a rectangular shape interrupts the regularity of the design and adds interest. *Photo 1–16*

Rectangles

Strips can be joined together and recut into rectangular shapes to create an easy border. Lynda Smith sewed strips together in fabrics that complement the framed Nine-patch blocks in her quilt. Units were cut into 7" lengths, and the sections were sewn together to make borders that fit the edges of the quilt. Solid blocks were used in the corners. *Photo 1–17*

NINE-PATCH HARVEST, by Lynda Smith, Paducah, Kentucky.
Quilted by Sarah Moss.

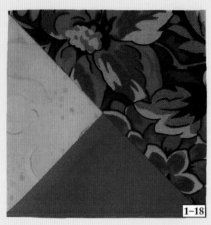

Split half-square

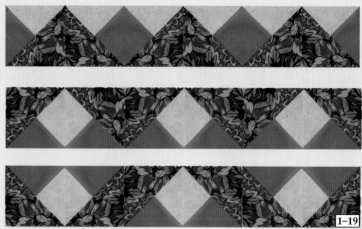

Split half-squares in pieced units

Divided Squares

Split half-squares can be used to create ribbon-like borders. This versatile pieced unit can be arranged to create a variety of border designs. *Photos 1–18 & 1–19*

Triangles

The bias lines of triangles can add motion to a border. Sometimes a sawtooth or dogtooth border can be just the addition a quilt needs. Whether you use half-square or isosceles triangles, the color placement can completely change the look of the border. *Photo 1–20*

LOVELY PINK *by Lynda Smith. Machine quilted by Sally Terry.*
Adapted from VICTORIAN ROSE, *A Garden of Quilts* by Mary Elizabeth Johnson, Oxmoor House *(1984).*

Pieced Blocks

Using a design element from the center of the quilt as part of the borders helps to tie the elements of the quilt together. In CRESSIDA, the Quilt Mavens, Deb Karasik and Janet Mednick, used the pieced spiky-point blocks in both the center and borders. *Photo 1–21*

1–21

CRESSIDA, by the Quilt Mavens, Deb Karasik and Janet Mednick, San Francisco, California

1–22

Stretching design into border

Stretching Design into Border

Continuing a portion of the quilt center into the border can complete a design element and create an interesting border. *Photo 1–22*

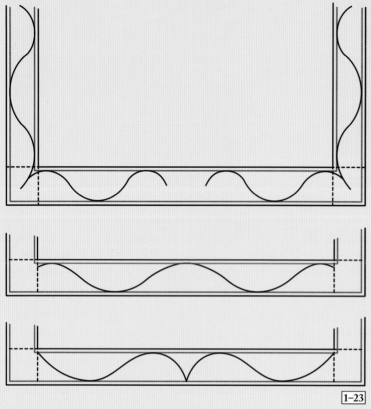

Flexibility is a key when designing appliquéd borders.

1–23

Appliquéd Borders

Creating an appliquéd design that is in proportion to the quilt center, making it fit the edges, and turning the corners are the challenges of making appliquéd borders. Appliquéd borders can be designed to travel in one direction around the quilt, to reverse at the midpoint of each border, or to flow out from the corners. The design can also begin at a miter or corner square and flow to the next corner, requiring a plain corner or design to fill it. Flexibility is definitely a key when designing appliquéd borders. Flowers, vines, and other designs from nature let you use your own creativity in stitching appliquéd borders. *Photo 1–23*

Vines can be used in a variety of ways, from zigzags to shallow curves. The design looks best if it covers the width of the border, leaving a narrow margin of ½" to 1" at each edge. The width of the margin will depend on the width of the border. The narrower the border, the narrower the margin should be. If you leave a large margin on each side of the border, plan to fill that space with a quilting design or background quilting to keep from getting those large puffy areas that make your quilt look unfinished. *Photo 1–24*

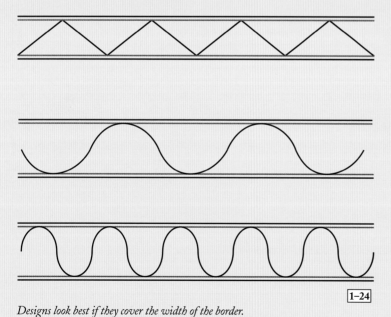

1–24

Designs look best if they cover the width of the border.

Undulating vines have long been used as border designs. They can be as simple or complex as you like. These designs can be used as a simple vine with berries, simple flowers, flowers and leaves, or a complex floral design. *Photo 1–25*

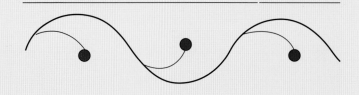

Festoons (swags) of fruit tied with leaves and flowers were popular during the Roman Renaissance and later periods. Originally, real fruit was hung as decoration on the friezes of temples. Later, fruit was included as part of the architecture of the building. Swags can be designed as single pieces, divided either horizontally or vertically, scalloped, or overlapped. The swag design can be simple, with straight edges, or it can have straight edges on the inside with scallops facing the outer edges of the quilt. The swags can be a single piece of fabric, or two or three fabrics can be used for the swags.

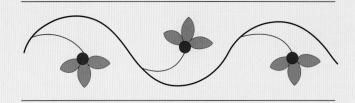

Sometimes, a swag design might not meet exactly at the edge of the corner square. If this happens, extend the design to fit the space and connect the swags on the two sides or add a design element in the center of each border to help fill the space. Adding a flower, bow, or other motif where the swags meet will cover any inaccuracies. *Photo 1–26*

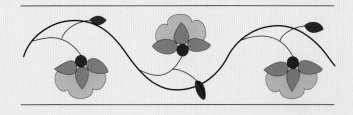

If an appliquéd border is used with a pieced quilt center, using some of the fabrics from the blocks in the appliqué will help to tie the borders to the center part of the quilt.

1–26

Swag with motif

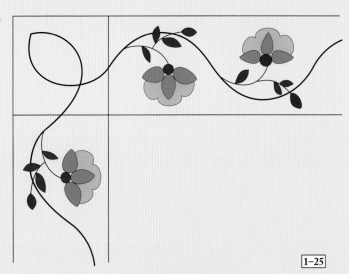

1–25

Undulating vines can be as simple or complex as you like.

Striped border. STARS ON SAFARI, *by the author.*
Quilted by Irene Reising.

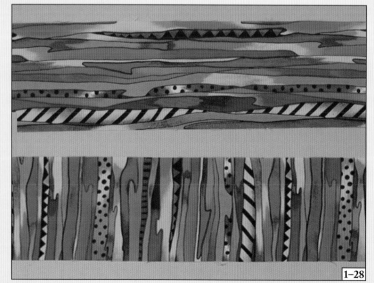

Stripes: length and width cuts

Striped Borders

Using striped fabrics for borders can add interest without having to piece or appliqué the borders. Usually the design is matched at mitered corners to continue the flow of the border design. Sometimes, a narrow band will need to be added to the quilt top so that the print can be matched. Measure the repeat of the stripe and make the border a multiple of that dimension. For example, if the stripe repeat measures 1¼", make the finished size of the border 1¼", 2½", or 3¾" so the repeat will meet properly in the corners. Don't forget to add seam allowances beyond the repeat to both long edges. There is always some waste when working with stripes because you need to cut into the next stripe for the seam allowances. *Photo 1–27*

When you cut stripes across the width of the fabric, you can make squares or rectangles, depending on how wide you cut the pieces. When you want to match miters in the corners, the length of the border will need to be in measurements of the width of the strips to make the stripes match at the corners. If your quilt is not the size you need, simply add another border to enlarge the quilt to the correct size before adding the striped border. Experiment by cutting stripes across the fabric width or down the length. *Photo 1–28*

Corner Treatments

Once you have decided on a border design, the next question is how to turn the corners. Pieced designs are perhaps easier than appliquéd borders because you can place a block in the corner to continue the design and use the corner blocks to help you align and pin the border to the quilt. That corner block can be plain, a pieced design from the interior of the quilt, or another design that helps to carry the eye around the corner. Of course, some quilters prefer different designs on every border, and in that case, there may be no common corner blocks

The corner treatment in an appliquéd border can be handled in several ways. The corner design can be a continuation of the design of the border. It can have a circular, elliptical, triangular, or heart shape to connect the designs. Or, the corners can be left blank (no design) to make the other part of the border design more important. *Photo 1–29*

Stitching Corners

How to stitch the corners of the quilt borders is another design decision. Corners can be squared, mitered, shaped, or even split.

Corner Squares

When plain or pieced squares are added to the border corners, they are called "corner squares." The top, bottom, and side borders are cut to fit their respective edges. The corner squares are added to either the top and bottom or the side borders before those two borders are added to the quilt. The squares should be the required finished size plus ½" seam allowances. *Photos 1–30 & 1–31*

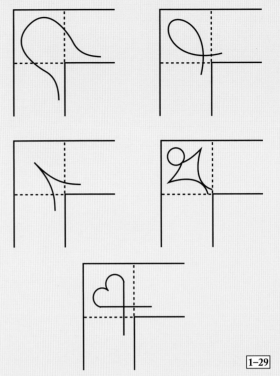

1–29

Variety of corner treatments.

1–30

Plain corner block of NINE-PATCH HARVEST (See the full quilt on page 11.)

1–31

MP/MQ, by Patty Winters. Collection of the author.

Faux mitered corner in busy print

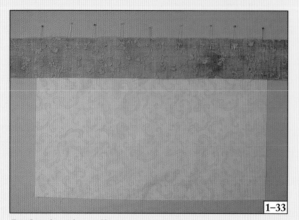
Border pinned to quilt

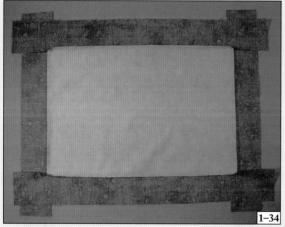
Border laid out for marking

Faux Mitered Corners

You can use a half-square in the corner to give the look of a mitered corner. Simply turn the half-square's diagonal seam so that it points toward the corner. This method works well with an allover print so the seams are not so obvious where you join the corner squares with the borders. *Photo 1–32*

Mitered Corners

Mitered corners are often used when bands, multiple bands, or appliquéd borders are added. When the design is being carried around the corner, as in appliqué, one less seam is involved if you use a miter in the corner. It is important that the borders be cut accurately to fit the edges of the quilt top so the miters will lie flat. Excess fabric at the corners can make what are called "dog-eared corners," ones that stick up and out from the quilt.

Sewing Borders to the Quilt

To sew the borders to your quilt, find and mark the center of the quilt edge and the border strip. Pin the centers, right sides together. Lay the quilt and border out flat and continue pinning from the center to the edges. Place the last pin ¼" from the edges of the quilt. *Photo 1–33*

You will start and stop sewing ¼" from the edges of the quilt. Do *not* sew into the seam allowances. Sew all four borders to the quilt. You can save some time by pinning two opposite borders, sewing them to the quilt, and then pin and sew the remaining two borders to the quilt.

Marking the Miters

Mitered corners are not hard to make, but they do require knowing how to mark the 45-degree angle.

After all four borders have been sewn to the quilt, lay the quilt, wrong side up. Place one border over the other. *Photo 1–34*

Lay your ruler, aligning the 45-degree angle on the seam line of the strip you are marking. Place the tip of your marking pencil in the last stitch and slide the ruler up to the pencil (double check that the 45-degree angle is still on the seam line) and carefully draw the angle on your border. *Photo 1–35*

Place the other border strip on top and repeat the process. Depending on how the angles are marked on your ruler, you may have to flip your ruler over to the back to align the angle.

Always make sure you are using the 45-degree angle. It is very easy to use 30 degrees or 60 degrees if you are not paying attention. Double-check the angle each time before you draw. To paraphrase an old saying: Measure twice, mark once!

Now that you have the angles marked, you are ready to sew them. Fold the quilt as shown, aligning the raw edges of the border. *Photo 1–36*

Starting at the outer edge, place a straight pin (a positioning pin) through the two layers of the border on the drawn line. Look at the bottom layer to see if this positioning pin is on the line. If not, simply lift the bottom layer and move the fabric until you can align the pin on the line. *Photo 1–37*

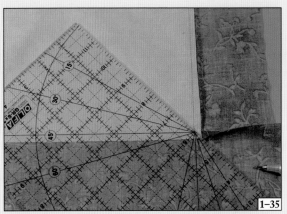

Position a 45-degree angle on the seam line to mark the miter.

Align the raw edges of the border.

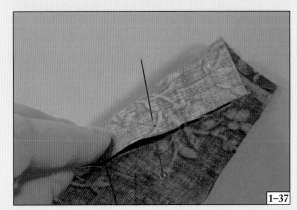

Place a positioning pin on the drawn line.

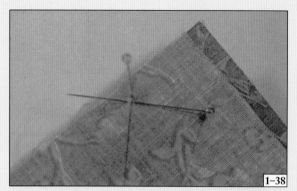

Secure the two layers together with a second pin.

Place pins every couple of inches along the drawn miter.

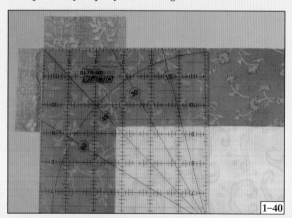

Check miter and trim excess fabric.

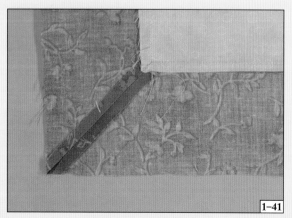

Press seam open and trim excess fabric.

Once you have the drawn lines aligned with the positioning pin, use another pin to secure the two layers together. Do not use the positioning pin to secure the layers. If you twist that pin, the bottom layer will move and your miter lines will no longer be aligned. *Photo 1–38*

Repeat this process, placing a pin every couple of inches along the drawn miter. *Photo 1–39*

Sewing the Miters
Begin sewing from the corner of the quilt to the edge of the border. After sewing the miter, press the seam open before trimming. Check your miter, and if you are pleased with it, then trim the excess fabric even with the edges of the border. *Photo 1–40*

By pressing the seam allowances open, it reduces the bulk in the corners of your quilt. Continue pinning and sewing the remaining mitered corners of your borders. *Photos 1–41 & 1–42*

If you have multiple bands in your border, place the first positioning pin where the seams join. To keep the layers of fabric from shifting, place a pin *on both sides* of the positioning pin. *Photo 1–43*

May you stitch many beautiful miters on your quilts! You now know how to make four of them on every quilt.

Special Corners
For some quilts, a shape other than a squared corner would look better. For a softer look, try rounded or curvy corners. Beds with corner posts will be easier to make with split corners on a quilt.

Shaped Corners
Some designs call for the corners to be rounded. An easy way to make that curve is to lay a large dinner plate in the corner and draw around it. Remember to use a bias binding if you choose a curved edge for your quilt. *Photo 1–44*

Split Corners
Beds with corner posts require that the bottom corners of the quilt be split to fit the posts at the end of the bed. To do this, determine the drop on the side of the bed and cut out a square from both bottom corners to that measurement. Then the bottom of the quilt will fit between the bedposts, and the sides will drop neatly over the edges. *Photo 1–45*

Bias-Cut Borders

Use a variety of colors from the center of your quilt to make a bias-cut border for the edge treatment. This is a good way to bring the colors from the center to the edge of your quilt. For variety, change the width of the strips or the amount of the colors used.

For example, for 2" finished border strips, cut two strips (2½" x 44") of each color. Cut each of these strips in half so you have eight 2½" x 22" strips. For wider borders, you may need to keep your strips the full width of the fabric.

ßArrange the strips in the order you want to sew the colors together. *Photo 1–46*

Completed miterd corner

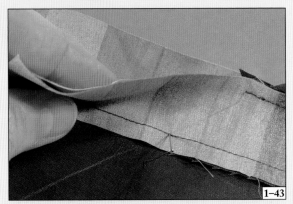

Multiple-band border

Helpline

Mitered Border Calculator

To determine the size to cut your borders for mitering, refer to the following formula and illustrated example:

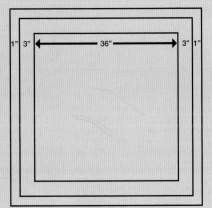

Finished length of quilt edge + 2x the finished width of the border + 2" for seam allowances and a fudge factor. Draw a sketch of your quilt to help you with your calculations.

Border length: 36" (body) + 6" (2 border widths) + 2" (seam allowance and fudge factor, 1" on each side) = 44" cut border length

Border width: 3" (finished border width) + ½" (seam allowances) = 3 ½" cut border width

For this square quilt, all four borders would be cut 3½" x 44".

If your quilt is rectangular, use this same formula to calculate the cut size of the other two borders.

A curved corner drawn using a dinner plate

Split corner detail

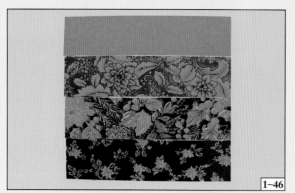

Arrange strips in color order.

Draw 45-degree angled lines.

Cut the bias border.

Multicolored binding

Offset each strip by 2" (the finished width of the strip). Sew the strips together, using a ¼" seam allowance.

Align the 45-degree angle on the ruler along one of the seams. Draw 45-degree angled lines across the pieced section, spacing the lines 2" apart. Number the lines at the top and bottom. Each line will have the same number at both ends. *Photo 1–47*

Matching the numberred edges, right sides together, align strip 1 to 2, 2 to 3, etc. Sew with a ¼" seam to make a tube.

Cut on the drawn lines to create a bias-cut border. *Photo 1–48*

This bias-strip method can also be used to make a multicolored binding. *Photo 1–49*

Helpline

Stablize the Edges of Your Quilt

Anytime you have bias on the edges of the quilt body, you will want to stabilize the quilt by adding a straight-of-grain border. Especially if the quilt is a wallhanging, the straight-of-grain border will help keep the edges from sagging after the quilt has been hanging on a wall for a while.

If you are paper piecing blocks for your quilt (like the WINDMILL – TWISTED LOG CABIN quilt on page 66), the edges of the blocks are often cut off-grain when they are trimmed, and that creates the need for a straight-of-grain border.

You can cut straight-of-grain borders across the width or length of the fabric. There will be less stretch in the fabric when you cut the borders on the length (selvage edge) of the fabric.

Sewing additional series of rectangles on your strip before trimming will allow you to use the section you cut off to begin the next border.

Braided Borders

When you have made a quilt with strips of fabric, a fun way to use them is to make a braided border. This technique is similar to sewing an offset Log Cabin block. You start with a square and continue adding strips on just two sides of the square.

Cut your strips into 2½" x 6" rectangles.

Cut one 2½" square. Sew the square to the side of one rectangle. *Photo 1–50*

Continue sewing strips on adjoining sides, matching the top edge of the last strip you stitched. *Photo 1–51*

When your strip is long enough to fit the quilt, cut the border to fit the edge of the quilt and trim the points on each side of the border to give you a straight edge. Be sure to include ¼" on each side for seam allowances. *Photos 1–52 & 1–53*

Handle these borders carefully. Because you have bias on the edges of the borders, they will be stretchy. Add some extra pins along the edge to help avoid stretching these edges as you sew.

Helpline

Pressing Seams

When pressing seams that go in opposite directions, use the edge of your ironing board. Press the first row and let it hang over the edge. Now the second row can be pressed without having the first row in your way.

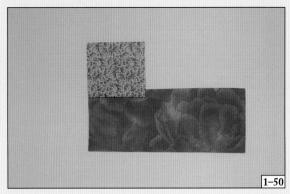

Sew square to the side of rectangle.

Continue sewing strips on adjoining sides.

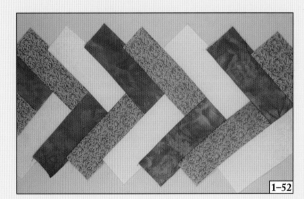

Cut border length to fit quilt.

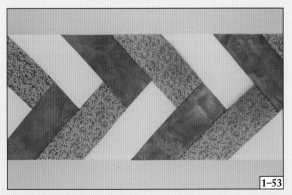

Trim border to fit the quilt edge.

Finishing Touches

There is a variety of finishing touches that can be added to the borders or edges of your quilts to make them extra special. Try adding piping. It can be flat, corded, double, or triple. Rickrack is the rage again and can easily be inserted into borders or binding. Couched threads can be sophisticated, fun, and funky, or they can be added just for some extra color. Stitches on your sewing machine can be used to make beautiful shell-scalloped piping. Other edge treatments include prairie points, scallops, dogtooth edges, and shark's teeth. Try one of these touches to finish the edges of your quilts.

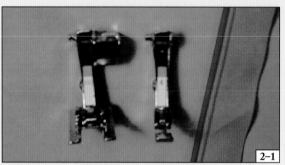

Sample of open-toe and zipper feet (Bernina)

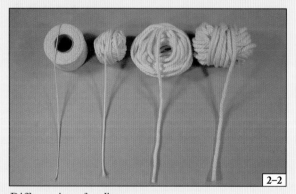

Different sizes of cording

Flat piping basted to quilt

Adding Piping

Piping can be used to separate borders or as an edge treatment in the binding. Mini piping can be used to outline appliqué. Piping can be flat, corded, couched, or decorated. There are several varieties of specialty feet that can be used for making piping. Try your zipper foot, an open-toed foot with a space on the bottom of the foot to allow the fabric to pass freely, or a cording foot if you have one for your machine. *Photo 2–1*

A variety of fillers can be used for piping: cotton string, perle cotton, yarn, cotton cord, or rattail cord. The filler cord should be preshrunk because it may shrink more than the cotton fabric used in your quilt. *Photo 2–2*

To preshrink the filler, place the cord in a zippered lingerie bag and soak in warm water. Roll the bag in a bath towel to remove excess moisture and hang the bag to air dry.

Making Piping Strips

Piping can be made from straight-of-grain strips or bias strips (preferred by the author). Straight-grain piping must be used on straight edges. Curved edges require piping made from bias strips. Bias fabric also adds interesting design elements when cut from stripes or other directional prints.

Flat Piping

You can add a decorative flat piping strip into any seam. A bias strip will give you more flexibility than one cut on the straight of grain. Determine the width you want the flat piping to be. A width of ¼" or ⅜" seems to be the most common. A wider strip may be harder to keep lying flat. Your strips should be cut twice the desired finished width plus ½" for seam allowances. Cut strips in lengths to fit all four sides of your quilt. Fold each strip in half along its length, wrong sides together, and baste the flat piping to the edges of the quilt with a scant ¼" seam. Basting will keep the layers from shifting when you sew the next border on the quilt. *Photo 2–3*

At the corners, you can either overlap the piping *(Photo 2–4)*, or you can sew piping strips to two opposite sides of the quilt then add the top and bottom piping and create mitered corners, as follows: On the top and bottom, place a pin the length of the piping at both ends of the strip. Start and stop sewing at these pins. For example, if your piping measures ½" folded, then place the pins ½" from each end of the quilt as your starting and stopping points. Fold the ends under to form a 45-degree corner and blind stitch the corners closed.

Flat piping can also be attached by folding the corners in the same manner as you would apply binding to the edge of the quilt (see Sewing the Binding on page 42). Instead of wrapping the piping over the edge, you would just tack the mitered corners and keep the piping flat.

Now, if you want to have fun with flat piping, try tacking it back every couple of inches with a decorative flower stitch or perhaps a bead, for a three-dimensional look. *Photo 2–5*

Corded Piping

Cut bias strips at least 1" wide for mini-corded piping, such as perle cotton or other similar threads. For piping made by covering cording or yarns, cut the strips at least 1" wider than the finished width of the piping. Try using 1½" wide strips. You can always trim the piping again after it is stitched. It is always easier to sew piping if you have some extra width in the fabric strip. After making the piping, the seam allowance should be trimmed to ¼".

If you want to miter the corners where the piping meets, stop sewing at least the width of the piped strip from each corner. This will give you room to fold the 45-degree angles. *Photo 2–6*

Stitching Piping

Make the piping by laying a filler cord on the wrong side of a bias strip. Fold the fabric, wrong sides together, matching the raw edges of the strip. There are several types of feet for the sewing machine that can be used to stitch the cording into place. A zipper foot is a good choice. You can adjust the needle position on many machines to stitch close to, but not through, the cording. You could also use a pintuck, an open toe, or cording foot. Adjust the needle position as necessary.

Use your fingers in front of the foot to push the cord against the fold of the fabric and guide the zipper foot as close as possible to the cording. *Photo 2–7*

Overlapped flat piping

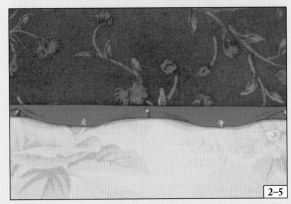
Tacking flat piping with decorative stitch

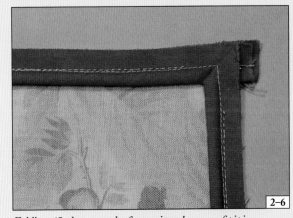
Folding 45-degree angles for a mitered corner of piping

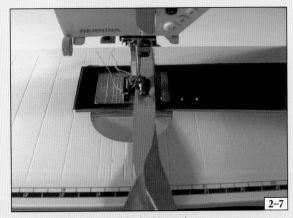
Stitching the cording inside the bias strip

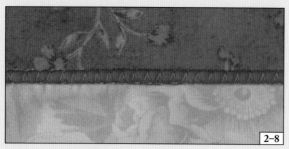

Decorative stitching over the corded piping

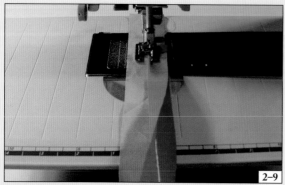

For double piping, layer two fabrics and stitch cording inside the top layer.

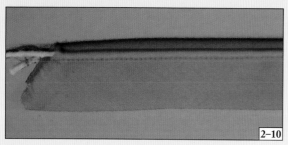

Cord stitched inside second strip, untrimmed

Stitch the piping to the binding.

Decorative Piping

Try using decorative stitches on your sewing machine to stitch the cording inside the bias strip. Adjust the stitch width so the needle stitches off the folded edge of the bias strip and over the cording. *Photo 2–8*

Piped Binding

The piping will appear more uniform if you stitch the piping to the binding before stitching the binding to the quilt.

Fold the binding in half, wrong sides together, and press. Take care not to stretch the binding if you are using bias. This fold line, on the right side of the binding, is the guide for aligning the folded edge of the piping.

Double Piping

You can make a double- or triple-piped binding. Using bias strips to make the piping will give these piped edges more flexibility. Double and triple piping works best inserted into straight seams. They do not work as well on curved seams.

To make double piping, cut 1½" to 2" wide strips of bias fabric in a length that fits the perimeter of the quilt plus 12" for corners. It is much easier to work with strips that are slightly wider than necessary so you have some material to hang on to as you sew. You can always trim the seam allowances later.

Lay the two colors of strips right sides together, matching the raw edges. Begin by inserting the cording in the color lying on top. Fold the raw edges of this strip together and stitch close to the cording but not completely snug against the cording. Sew along the length of the piping strip through all the layers. *Photo 2–9*

Now, you are ready to insert the second piping. Because the two layers are held together by the stitching for the first piping, you can just fold over the second strip to encase the second cording. This time adjust your needle position one click to the left and stitch the cording inside the second strip. Voilà! Wasn't that a slick way to quickly make a double piping? Trim the seam allowances to ¼" to reduce bulk as you insert this unit between other layers. *Photo 2–10*

To use the double piping in the binding, fold the binding in half lengthwise, wrong sides together, and press. Align the piped unit with the folded edge on the fold line of the binding strip. Stitch the piping to the binding. *Photo 2–11*

More Decorative Ideas

Add decorative touches by using commercially available trims like rickrack or other trims. Special threads can be couched using decorative machine stitches. Make your own trims like the shell-scalloped piping. Try out other stiches to create your own unique trims.

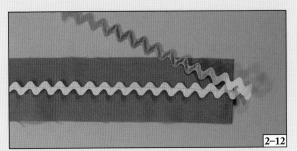

Rickrack aligned down the center of binding

Rickrack

To attach rickrack to your binding, fold the binding in half lengthwise, wrong sides together, and press. Take care not to stretch the binding if you are using bias. This fold line on the right side of the binding is the guide for aligning the center of your rickrack. Open the binding and tack the rickrack in place with a line of fabric glue on one side of the center fold of the binding. *Photo 2–12*

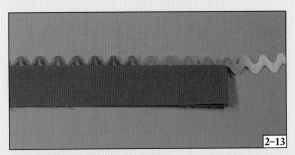

Folded binding with rickrack edge

Turn the binding over and use a straight stitch to sew down the fold line of the binding. Refold the binding, matching the raw edges. Half of the rickrack will extend beyond the folded edge of the binding. *Photo 2–13*

Try stitching a decorative stitch down the center of the rickrack and use that stitching to couch the rickrack to the quilt. For a fun addition to a child's quilt, add rickrack, in his or her favorite colors, to sashing or borders.

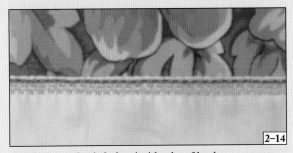

Couched threads stitched on inside edge of border

Couching

In addition to piping, many other types of decorative threads, ribbons, cords, etc., can be laid on a seam line and couched in place by using a monofilament thread and a zigzag or decorative stitch. Use the monofilament thread as the upper thread, and regular sewing or bobbin thread in the bobbin. Use a foot that enables you to see the placement of the threads on the seam line. There are a number of couching feet available that have a hole to run the couching thread through to keep it in position. You may need to adjust the needle to make sure you are covering the threads. *Photo 2–14*

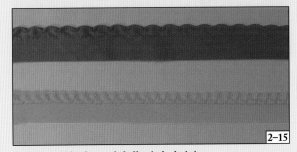

Samples of blanket and shell-stitched piping

Shell-Scalloped Piping

A shell-shaped piping adds a soft edge to a border or binding. Use soft fabrics, like fine cotton, silk, or batiste, to get the best shell effect. To make shell-scalloped piping, cut bias strips 2" wide and fold the strips in half lengthwise, wrong sides together. Press. Sew a shell stitch or a blanket stitch, positioning it so the swing of the stitch falls just off the edge of the fold. Set the stitch width as wide as possible for your sewing machine. Tighten the tension on your machine. If your normal tension is 4, set the tension at 6–8. The tighter tension will pull the fabric up to form the shells. Trim the seam allowances to ¼". *Photos 2–15 & 2–16*

Shell-stitched piping inserted between quilt top and border

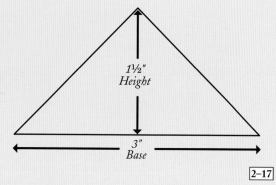

Height of prairie point is half of the base.

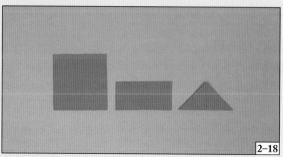

Rectangle fold

Insert points 1" larger between a row of prairie points.

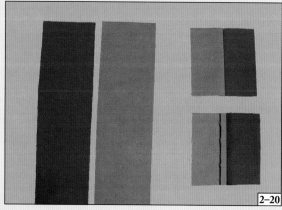

Two-color rectangle fold

Edge Treatments

While you can finish the edge of your quilt with plain borders and a binding, there are a number of decorative treatments that can make your quilt extra special. Try adding prairie points, scallops, shark's teeth, dog-teeth, or piping before you add that final binding to the edge of your quilt.

Prairie Points

Prairie points can be inserted on the edges of blocks, in borders, or at the edge of a quilt. Even though prairie points look similar to dogteeth and shark's teeth (see pages 34 and 35), only the prairie points have finished edges, so they can be inserted anywhere.

To make prairie points that will fit your quilt perfectly, see how to fold adding-machine tape as shown in the Making Borders Fit section on page 5. Measure from one fold to the next to find the finished size of the base of a point. Add ½" to that measurement for seam allowances. The height of the prairie point will be one-half the finished size of the base. *Diagram 2–17*

Rectangle Fold

A prairie point can be made by folding a square in half to form a rectangle. Then, turn the folded corners down so the raw edges meet. *Photo 2–18*

When placing prairie points on the edge of your quilt, be sure to overlap them about ¼" so they will butt against each other when sewn. As a variation, after making the first set of prairie points, make a second set from squares that are 1" larger than the first set. Each of these larger prairie points will fit behind two of the first points. *Photo 2–19*

Two-color Rectangle Fold

Two-color prairie points can be made by sewing together two different strips of fabric. To determine the width to cut each strip, refer to your folded adding-machine tape and divide the measurement from one fold to the next by 2, then add ½" for seam allowances. For example, if the finished base of the point is 2", 2" ÷ 2 = 1" + ½" for seam allowances = 1½" cut width for each of the two colors of strips. Sew the two strips, right sides together, on one long side. Cut the two-color strip into squares and fold as shown for the rectangle fold. *Photo 2–20*

Piped Prairie Points

Piped prairie points are made by first stitching a bias-piped strip between two straight-of-grain strips in another color. You will need to determine the size to make each prairie point. (See how to fold adding-machine tape as shown in the Making Borders Fit section on page 5.) Measure one fold of your adding machine tape to determine the base of each prairie point. Count the number of folds in your strip for both the top, bottom, and the sides to determine the number of prairie points you will need.

Cut strips for the prairie points. You will need two strips of fabric for the points for each quilt edge. The length of the strips will equal the number of points per edge times the measurement for one fold of your adding machine tape. These strips will be cut on the straight of grain. The piping will be stitched between the two fabrics.

To determine the width to cut each strip, divide the measurement from one fold to the next by 2 and add ½" for seam allowances; i.e., if the finished base of the point (fold-to-fold measurement) is 2", then 2" ÷ 2 = 1" + ½" for seam allowances = 1½", which is the cut width for each of the two strips.

Cut strips for the piping. Cut a 1" *bias* strip the length of the fabric for the prairie points for each edge of the quilt. (See Adding Piping on page 24.) Stitch a very small cording (a small yarn would be a good choice) inside the folded bias strip. Trim the seam allowances of the piping to ¼".

Sew the piping. Lay the piping on one of the fabric strips, right sides together, matching the raw edges. Use a cording or buttonhole foot to stitch these layers together. Place the second strip of fabric right sides together with the previously sewn piping and fabric strip. (Place the sewn strip on top so you can follow the previous stitching line.) Stitch slightly closer to the cording this time. By sewing the piping to one strip first and then sewing the second strip to that unit, you will have less shifting of the fabrics. *Photo 2–21*

Press the strips open. With the piping on top, cut the strips into squares, using the measurement from folding the freezer paper. Use the rectangle-fold method to turn the squares into prairie points. *Photo 2–22*

Triangle Fold
You can also make prairie points from squares that are folded from corner to corner and then folded to the opposite corner to form the point. *Photo 2–23*

These points can be slipped inside one another for a staggered look. An easy way to space these prairie points uniformly is to fold back one point and lay the next point halfway inside the first point. *Photos 2–24 & 2–25*

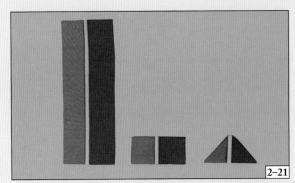
Piped prairie points

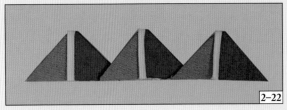
Rectangle fold and overlap

Triangle-folded prairie points

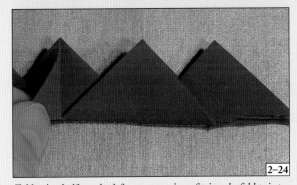
Fold point halfway back for even spacing of triangle-fold points.

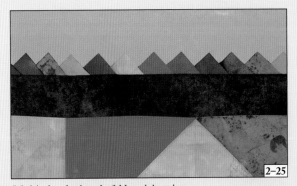
Multicolored triangle-fold prairie points

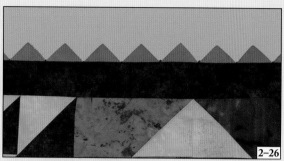

Prairie points overlap to make continuous Vs and points.

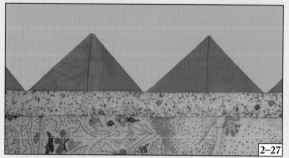

Binding is folded entirely to the back.

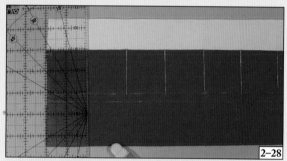

Mark off segments on one side of the fold.

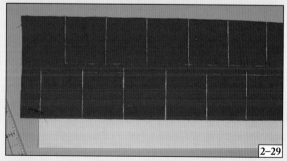

Mark the opposite side beginning with one-half segment.

Cut on the marked lines.

Sewing Points to Quilt

Select which side of the prairie points you want facing up, the smooth side or the folded side. Pin and baste the prairie points in place on the quilt top. The individual prairie points should overlap within the ¼" seam allowance. *Photo 2–26*

Stitch the points to the quilt edge. A single narrow binding can be applied and turned completely to the back of the quilt, or simply turn under the backing fabric to meet the stitching line of the prairie points. *Photo 2–27*

Continuous-Band Points

There are some advantages to making prairie points in a continuous band. They are evenly spaced, and they all turn out the same size. This method is fast and easy.

You begin by determining the size of prairie point needed to fit the edge of your quilt. (Refer to Making Borders Fit on page 5.)

To determine the size to cut the width of the continuous strip, double the size required to make one prairie point. This measurement is doubled because your strip is actually making a double row of prairie points. Add 1" to that measurement for seam allowances (that adds ½" for seam allowances for the points on each side). For example, if the finished size of the prairie point is 1½", add 1½" (one side) + 1½" (second side) + 1" (seam allowances) = 4" wide strip. The finished points will be 1½" at the base and ¾" in height.

To calculate the length of the strip, determine the finished length of the side of the quilt. If you measure the side of your quilt, it will include the ¼" seam allowance at each end. Subtract ½" from that measurement to give you the finished size of the quilt edge.

Prepare the continuous strip. Cut the fabric strip. Press it in half with wrong sides together. Mark off segments on one side of the fold. Use your folded adding-machine paper to divide it equally (see Making Borders Fit section on page 5). *Photo 2–28*

On the opposite side of the fold line, the first segment will be one-half of a segment. The remaining segments will be full. *Photo 2–29*

Cut the squares on the marked lines from the outer edge to the center fold. *Photo 2–30*

Fold the points. Work at the ironing board and press as you go. Turn the fabric strip wrong side up. Begin with the first section; fold the corner diagonally to form a triangle. To make the second fold, turn the corner down while aligning the cut edge with the fold of the strip. Place a pin to hold the prairie point closed. *Photo 2–31*

Fold the next prairie point on the opposite side of the strip. Fold the corner toward the previously folded prairie point as shown. *Photo 2–32*

Continue folding in this manner, alternating from side to side, until all of the points are folded and pinned. *Photo 2–33 & Photo 2–34*

To hold the points in place, machine stitch ⅛" from the raw edge of the points, removing pins as you go. Continue making strips for the other sides of your quilt. *Photo 2–35*

Sew the continuous strip. Pin the prairie point strip to the right side of the quilt top. In the event that the strip is too long or too short, you can cut off one point (you'll need to unstitch it at the base and unfold it to remove it). To add one point, simply cut a square, fold, and insert as needed.

To avoid excess bulk in the seam allowance, sew the points only to the quilt top and batting. This will allow you to trim the batting close to the stitching line. Fold the prairie points away from the quilt top. Fold the backing under along the seam line and stitch in place.

Fold to form triangle and press.

Fold prairie point on opposite side.

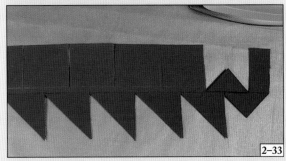
Continue folding points.

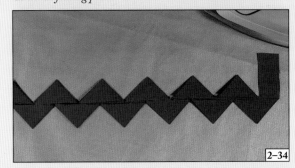
Points are folded on both sides of the strip.

Completed strip

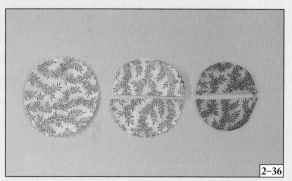

Scallops from circles

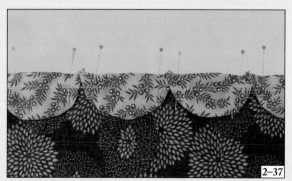

Scallops pinned in place

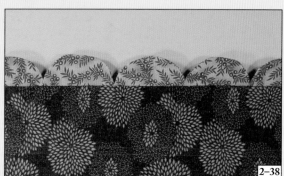

Finished scallops

More Edges

Edges don't have to be straight. Make the edge curved by adding individual or continuous scallops.

Scalloped Edges

A scalloped edge can add beauty and elegance to a quilt. The scallops can be made by creating individual circles or by stitching the scallop shapes on a strip of fabric.

To determine the size of the scallops, see Making Borders Fit on page 5 and fold a piece of adding-machine tape the finished length of the edge of the quilt. The division from one fold to the next will be the finished base of one scallop. Add ½" for seam allowances to the base dimension if you are making individual scallops.

Scallops from Circles

Make individual scallops and pin them to the edge of the quilt before adding the binding. To make the scallops, stitch two circles around their perimeters, right sides together. Cut them in half, clip the curves, and turn them right side out. *Photo 2–36*

Overlap the edges of the scallops ¼" from the raw edge so there will be no gaps between them when stitched. The seam allowances will overlap when they are properly pinned in place. *Photo 2–37*

It seems to work better to baste the scallops to the top of the quilt, then apply a narrow binding that wraps to the back of the quilt. This will make the scallops turn outward to become the edge of the quilt. Blind-stitch the binding on the quilt back. *Photo 2–38*

Scallops from Strips

Scallops from strips can face the center of the quilt, be inserted into a seam, or placed on the edge of a quilt. They can be doubled by layering two sets of scallops in two colors and staggered for added interest to the quilt edge. The advantage of this method is that you have more flexibility in the shapes of the scallops. They can be circles, ovals, or they can even be arranged like an undulating vine. They can also be free-form and not symmetrical.

To make scallops in a strip, you first stitch the scallop shape then attach it to the quilt. Determine the width of the strip by the depth of the scallop. The width of the strip should measure twice the finished depth of the scallop plus 2" for seam allowances and trimming. The strips can be straight of grain or bias. You will need to join strips as needed to fit the edge of the quilt. Fold the strip in half lengthwise, right sides together.

Because the scallop edge is only two layers of fabric, you may want to add some support to make it comparable to the weight of the quilt with batting. Cut a strip of lightweight fusible interfacing, lightweight batting, or another strip of fabric the same size as the folded strip. Press the interfacing (or use fabric glue on the fabric or batting) to adhere it to the wrong side of the folded strip. *Photo 2–39*

Iron the freezer paper to the wrong side of the folded fabric. Use 12 to 14 stitches per inch and straight stitch on the marked lines on the freezer paper. Remove the freezer paper. Trim the scallops with pinking shears to help grade the seam. Clip into the corners with scissors, making a Y at the seam line. *Photo 2–40*

Trim the seam allowance on the bottom edge to ¼". Turn the scallops right side out. Press.

Align the raw edge of the scallop strip with the raw edge of the quilt edge. Use a scant ¼" seam allowance to stitch the scallops to the edge of the quilt. On the back of the quilt turn the edge under ¼". Blindstitch the edge to the quilt back. *Photos 2–41 & 2–42*

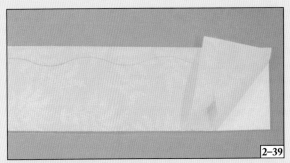
Draw circular shapes on freezer paper.

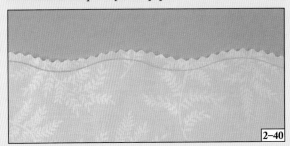
Trim the scallops with pinking shears to help grade the seam.

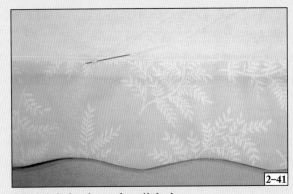
Blindstitch the edge on the quilt back.

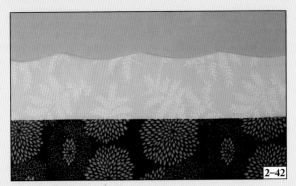
Scalloped edge

Insert the folded paper to mark the dogtooth divisions.

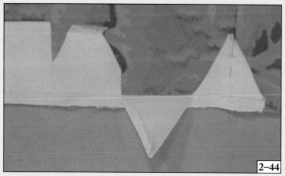

Fold the top edge under ¼".

Fold edges under and appliqué the dogtooth border.

Dogtooth Edges

The dogtooth edge usually is inserted at the border or quilt edge with the teeth pointing toward the center of the quilt, or on both edges of a border. It is usually appliquéd in place by hand or machine. A dogtooth border can also be made by piecing triangles together, or by using a foundation-pieced pattern that fits the edge of your quilt.

See Making Borders Fit on page 5 to and fold a piece of adding-machine tape to determine the size of the base for each dogtooth. To make the appliquéd dogtooth edge from a single strip of fabric, cut a 1½" wide strip of fabric. Baste the strip to the edge of the quilt using a scant ¼" seam allowance. Mark and cut slits by using the spacing as determined when you folded the adding-machine tape. You can just insert the folded paper under the basted fabric to use as a guide to make the slits. *Photo 2-43*

Do not cut beyond the basting stitches, leaving the seam allowance uncut. Turn the top edge under ¼". *Photo 2-44*

Fold in one edge from the point to the bottom of the cut and appliqué. Fold the other edge, tucking fabric under the point and continue appliquéing the dogtooth in place. *Photo 2-45*

What is the difference between dogtooth edges and shark's teeth? Shark's teeth are made by folding the fabric at 45-degree angles. A dogtooth has angles that are more or less than 45 degrees. These angles require folding the tip under and appliquéing the edges in place. If you want a finished edge or three-dimensional points, you need to use prairie points. All three of these edge treatments are somewhat similar in style on a quilt, but each has its own unique look and stitching method.

Shark's Teeth

The shark's tooth border is one of the most versatile border styles. It can be used as a single row or as multiple rows in different colors. It can be mirror-imaged in different colors, and mirror-imaged rows of teeth can have a narrow or wide strip between the rows. The extra border width between rows makes space for a beautiful appliquéd or quilted design.

A shark's tooth is scaled so that the finished height of the tooth is half the width of the base. For instance, if you want the teeth to be 1" high, the base will be 2". A large quilt can support larger teeth, so you might want to use a 2½" base for a bed-sized quilt. Wall-sized quilts will need a narrower base. Even miniature quilts look wonderful with very tiny shark's teeth on the border.

To divide the edge of your quilt into equal divisions, see Making Borders Fit on page 5. This folded adding-machine tape becomes your ruler to cut the teeth. so make sure the creases are good and sharp. *Photo 2–46*

Once you have the paper folded, you need to determine the width to cut the fabric strip to make the shark's teeth. Measure from one fold to the next. That is the finished size of the base of one tooth. Take that dimension and add ½" for seam allowances. This is the width to cut your strip. The length of the strip is the finished size of the edge of the quilt. (Measure the quilt edge and subtract ½" for the seam allowances.) Now you can test one tooth by cutting a square of fabric that is the width you need for the strip. Fold this square to make a rectangle and fold the cut edges to make a 45-degree angle. Lay it on the edge of the quilt to see if you think it is the right size, too large, or too small. You may need to make another series of folds in the freezer paper to make them smaller.

Making the shark's teeth: Fold the fabric strip in half lengthwise, wrong sides together. Press. Baste this folded strip to the quilt, sewing a scant ¼" in from each edge of the quilt. Remember, we are using the finished size of the edge of the quilt on this strip, so the strip will start and stop ¼" from each end of the quilt. Slide the folded paper under the fabric and pin in place. Use the folds of the paper and a fabric or chalk marker to mark the divisions on the fabric. Clip from the fold of the fabric to the basting line. *Photo 2–47*

Folding method 1: Fold the cut edges to form a 45-degree angle, folding the corners to meet on the back. Use fabric glue to hold the corners in place. *Photo 2–48*

Use the folded paper to divide the border equally.

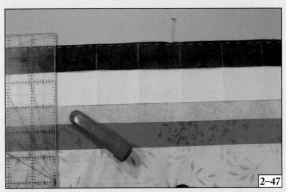

Use the folds of the paper to mark the divisions on the fabric.

Use fabric glue to hold the corners in place.

Two folds create teeth.

Appliqué the shark's teeth.

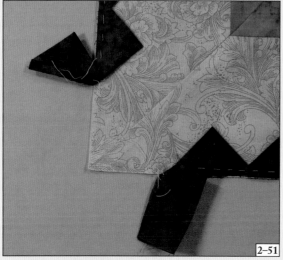

Cut off the last tooth on both sides of the corner.

Place a folded square across the corner for a neat finish.

Folding method 2: Fold the points. Use a pin to secure the center of the point. Push the right half to the inside with the tip of a needle. Finger crease. Repeat by pushing the left half to the inside and creasing. *Photo 2–49*

Appliqué the edges of the teeth in place. This can be appliquéd by hand or blindstitched by machine. At the inside of the V, take two or three short stitches to secure the raw edge. Repeat this procedure for the remaining teeth. *Photo 2-50*

If you want to make two rows of shark's teeth with a border in between, it's best to make the border width a multiple of the finished size of the shark's teeth. For instance, if the finished size (one division of your folded paper) is 2½", then the border needs to be two times, three times, or even four times that dimension. If you use three times, that would be 2½" x 3 = 7 ½". This is the finished size of the border, so you still need to add ½" for seam allowances. You would cut that border 8" wide. The length will depend on whether you are making butted or mitered corners.

Sometimes the corners of the teeth may not come out exactly as you might want them. There is a very easy solution. Just cut off the last two shark's teeth at the corner. *Photo 2-51*

Then measure from the last tooth to the corner of the quilt. Cut a square slightly larger than this measurement. Fold the square in half to form a triangle and align it with the last tooth on each side of the corner. Voilà! It comes out beautifully every time and no one is the wiser. That can be our secret. *Photo 2-52*

Binding can be added as usual along the edge, or you might want to wrap the binding completely to the back of the quilt to let the teeth become the final edge. For a bed quilt, it would be best to use binding because that is the first part of the quilt to wear out.

All About Bindings

The binding puts the finishing touch to the edge of a quilt. It is your last chance to add one more simple or spectacular element. For bed quilts, the binding is usually the first part to wear out, so it is important to make it sturdy and secure.

Edges without Binding

For those quilts that do not require a special edge treatment, the edges can be finished without binding by using one of the following methods. You will find that edges without binding are suitable for some projects, especially those quick and easy quilts. You need to be aware that edges without binding are not as strong and will probably not wear as well as edges with binding.

Stitch and Turn

Before quilting, layer the batting (either side up), the quilt top (right side up), and the backing (right side down). Pin the layers together around the edges. Stitch around the edges with a ¼" seam allowance, leaving a 12" opening on one side for turning the quilt. Turn the quilt right side out through the opening and blindstitch the opening closed. Quilt through all three layers.

This is a good method for quick quilts, and it is great for kids' quilts that are to be used and used up. A disadvantage to this method is that, by quilting after the edges are stitched, any excess fullness may result in some pleats or puckers on the surface of your quilt.

Front to Back

You can fold the front of the quilt to the back to encase the edges, as follows: Complete the quilting as usual. Trim the front of the quilt 1" larger than the batting and backing. Fold the front edge under ½" and fold it again, over the edge of the batting and backing, to the back. Stitch the folded edge, by hand or machine, to the quilt back.

Back to Front

Fold the backing to the front to encase the edges of the quilt, as follows: Complete the quilting as usual. Trim the backing 1" larger than the front and batting. Fold the backing over ½" and fold it again, over the batting and front edge, to the front. Stitch the folded edge to the front by hand or machine. This is a good time to use a decorative machine stitch to secure the edge. Or, couch a decorative thread as you stitch the fold in place.

Turning Both Edges

A fourth option is to turn the front and backing in and stitch the folded edges together. Begin by trimming the edges ½" beyond the quilting. Trim the batting ¼" narrower than the quilt top and backing. Fold the front over the batting. Fold the backing to meet the front edge. Blindstitch the folds together. This technique is sometimes used for irregular edges like those in Grandmother's Flower Garden or Double Wedding Ring. This method provides a weaker edge for a large quilt. Binding is preferable for a quilt that will be used and laundered regularly.

Edges with Binding

Binding helps to protect the edges of the quilt. It can be a single or double thickness, depending on the size of the quilt and how much wear the quilt will get.

Helpline

Binding Width Recommendations

Binding Finished Width	Strip Cut Width	Quilt Type
¼"	1½"	Miniature or small quilts
⅜"	2¼"	Wall or bed-sized quilts
½"	3"	Bed-sized quilts or special effects

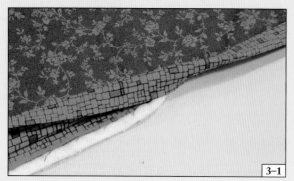

Cut batting and backing ¼" wider than the top.

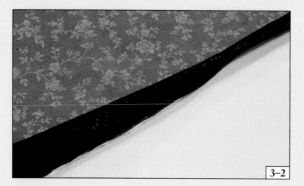

Cut even and use ½" seam allowance.

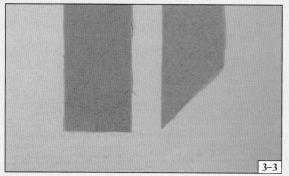

Straight-of-grain and bias binding

Use the chart on page 37 to determine the binding width that would be suitable for your quilt.

For finished binding wider than ¼", the edges of the quilt should be trimmed so that the batting and backing extend beyond the edge of the quilt front. This extra batting and backing will fill the binding so it wears better. For example, for a ½" finished binding, the batting and backing should extend ¼" beyond the quilt top. Align the binding with the edge of the quilt top and sew with a ¼" seam allowance. *Photo 3–1*

Another option would be to cut the three layers (top, batting, and backing) all the same and sew the binding on with a seam allowance that is the finished size of your binding. In the example of a ½" finished binding, you would then use a ½" seam allowance. *Photo 3–2*

You can even cut a narrow (¼" to ½", depending on the width of your binding) strip of batting to lay inside the binding as you fold it to the back, to make sure the binding is filled.

Straight of Grain or Bias?

Binding can be made either from strips cut on the straight of grain (usually across the width of the fabric) or on the bias (45-degree angle to the selvage).

The straight-of-grain binding will have long threads running the length of the binding, with only a few threads on the very edge of the quilt. If one of those edge threads gets broken, the edge will be weakened. However, if a bias strip is used for the binding and one thread gets broken, because there are so many more threads running along the edge of the quilt, little damage will have been done. Therefore, bias-cut binding will wear better than straight cut. *Photo 3–3*

Straight-Grain Binding Yardage

Finished Binding Width	Cut Width	Binding Yardage (linear inches)					
		⅜ yd	½ yd	⅝ yd	¾ yd	⅞ yd	1 yd
¼"	1½"	330	432	534	662	789	891
⅜"	2¼"	220	288	356	441	526	594
½"	3"	165	216	267	331	394	445

Straight-Grain Binding

Traditional French binding is made with a double layer of fabric, and it can be made from straight-grain or bias strips. It is usually sewn to the quilt top then hand stitched to the back of the quilt. This method provides a smoother finish on the top of the quilt. *Photo 3–4*

This binding can also be stitched completely by machine, and in that case, the binding is first sewn to the back of the quilt and then topstitched to the front. Decorative stitching can be used to secure the folded edge of the binding. Use some of those machine decorative stitches to add an additional design element to the front of your quilt. *Photo 3–5*

If you are making straight-grain French binding, make sure the strips are cut on the true straight of the grain or your binding may ripple. Try pulling a thread to get the true straight of grain.

Measuring for binding: For double-fold binding, the cut width should be at least six times the finished size, depending on the thickness of the fabric.

Before cutting any fabric to make binding, measure the edges of the quilt to see how many inches of binding you need. To this measurement, add 12" for turning and mitering the corners. The result is the number of linear inches needed.

Use the convenient table on page 38 to determine how much yardage you need to buy for your binding: Find your finished binding width in the first column. The second column gives you the cut width for your binding strips. Move across the remaining columns and find the linear inches needed. At the top of that column, you will find the yardage required for your binding.

If you need more binding than is shown in the chart, simply add yardage amounts together. For instance, if you need 700 linear inches for your ⅜"-wide binding, you could use two ⅝ yard pieces (356 linear inches each) to yield 712 linear inches (2 x ⅝ yd. = 1¼ yd.).

Bias Binding

Learn to make your own bias strips for binding or piping. After you've made a couple of bias bindings, you will find that they are really fairly easy to make. Making your own continuous bias strips gives you the option to use matching or contrasting fabric, or you can even create a special effect, like using stripes to form a barber-pole look on the edge of your quilt. *Photo 3–6*

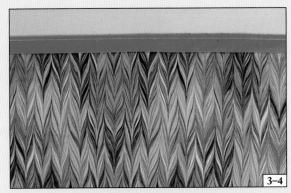

Stitch binding to the top of the quilt.

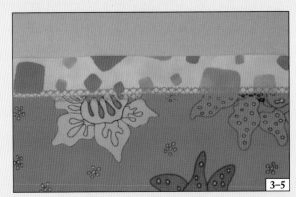

Use decorative stitches to topstitch the binding.

Use striped fabric for a barber-pole binding.

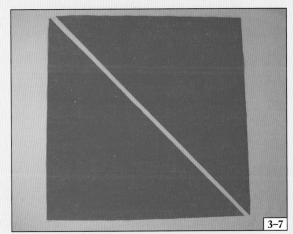

Make bias from a square of fabric.

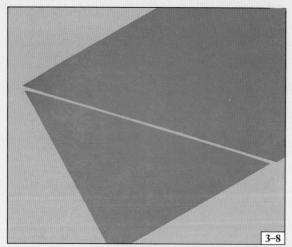

Make bias from a rectangle of fabric.

3–8

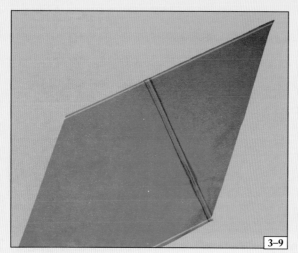

Sew one side of the triangle to the opposite side of the rectangle to form a parallelogram.

3–9

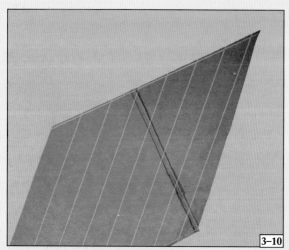

Space parallel lines the width you need to cut bias strips.

3–10

You can use a square or a rectangle to make continuous bias strips. Use the following formulas to determine the size of the square or rectangle needed for your bias binding:

Square: Multiply the strip length by the strip width to determine the amount (square inches) of fabric needed. Take the square root of that number and add the width of one cut strip for good measure. This is the size of the square you will need.

Example: If you need 330 linear inches of binding and the cut strip width is 1½", 330" x 1½" = 495 square inches. The square root of 495 is 22.25. Add 1½" (width of one strip) = 23.75". Therefore, you will need a square at least 23¾" to make your binding.

To find the yardage, divide 23.75 by 36"/ yard = .66 yards, rounded up to the nearest ⅛ yard = ¾ yard.

Rectangle: It's usually best to use a rectangle whose narrowest side is no shorter than 18". In the previous example, instead of taking the square root of 495, divide by 18", or whatever the width of your rectangle is, 495 ÷ 18" = 27.5". Add the strip width of 1½" as before, which = 29". You will need a rectangle 18" x 29" for your binding.

For the yardage, divide 18" by 36"/yard = .5, or ½ yard. You can add another ⅛ yard for insurance.

Starch the fabric to be used for cutting the binding strips. The starch makes it easier to cut the bias strips and to bind the quilt.

Trim the cut edges of your fabric to straighten them. Fold one edge over to meet an adjacent cut edge, forming a 45-degree angle. (The fold is on the bias.) Cut along the folded edge. You now have a triangle separate from the rest of the piece. *Photos 3–7 (square) & 3–8 (rectangle)*

Sew the edges together, as shown, with a ¼" seam allowance to form a parallelogram. Press the seam allowances open. Draw a ¼" seam allowance on both of the long raw edges. *Photo 3–9*

Starting on one of the long edges, draw lines across the fabric, spacing them the width you need to cut your bias strips. *Photo 3–10*

Place a pin on the first drawn line on the top edge of the marked fabric. This line will be matched to the edge on the bottom of the fabric. Using a positioning pin inserted at the seam line intersections, match the lines then pin in place. (Notice that the lines are offset.) There will be an extra tail when you reach the opposite end. The pinned fabric forms a tube. Sew this pinned seam and press the allowances open. *Photo 3–11*

Cut on the drawn lines. You can cut with scissors, or if your fabric tube will fit over the end of your ironing board, slide a rotary mat under the fabric and use a ruler and your rotary cutter to cut the continuous bias strip. You will have yards of continuous bias to use for binding or piping. *Photo 3–12*

There may be times when you want a strip of single-fold bias. Here's an easy way to fold this strip by using a long pin and your ironing board. Those long hatpins or corsage pins work great for this method. On the cover of your ironing board, stick the pin in and out, skip the distance for the width of your folded bias strip, and put the pin in and out again. *Photo 3–13*

Your bias strip should be twice the width of your finished binding. Push the strip of fabric under the pin. Sometimes cutting an angle on the end of the strip makes it easier to thread the fabric under the pin.

Pull the fabric through the pin, making sure the edges are folding in to meet in the center. Once they become evenly folded, press the strip as you pull it. Use one hand to pull, and press with the other. *Photo 3–14*

If you want double-fold bias, change the spacing of your pin to half the original space, and run the fabric through again. *Photo 3–15*

Helpline
Choosing Fabric for Outer Borders

If you are using pieced blocks in the borders, use them in an interior border. By using a single fabric for the outer border, you can trim as needed to make sure the corners are 90 degrees and the edges are straight. Try using a multicolored print for that outer border and any trimming will be less noticeable. This is especially helpful if you have your quilts machine quilted and you need to square up the quilt before adding the binding.

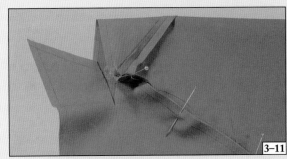

Use a positioning pin to match the drawn lines to sew the bias edges together.

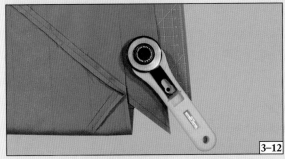

Cut yards and yards of bias.

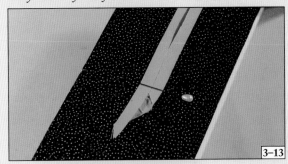

Stick a pin in and out on the ironing board.

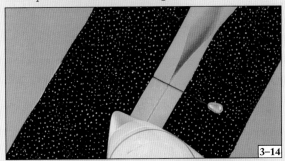

Pull the fabric under the pin and press as you pull.

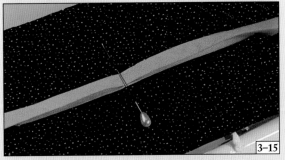

For double fold bias, move the pin and refold fabric.

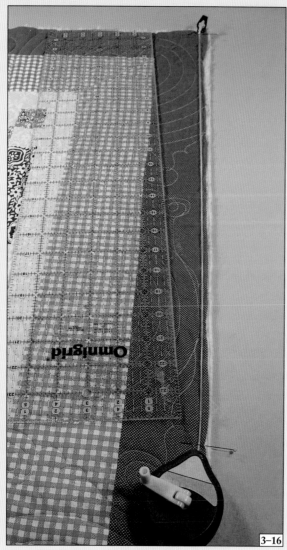

Use a chalk line to mark a straight edge on a quilt.

3–16

Helpline
Tips for Piped Binding

Use a fabric glue stick to tack the piping in place on the right side of the binding before you start sewing. Stitch the piping to the binding by using the previous stitching line as a guide.

If you can change your needle position on your sewing machine, move the needle one click closer to the cording to make sure you cover the original stitching line. Press the binding in half along the stitching line.

Trimming the Edges

After you have quilted the layers, it is time to trim the edges of the quilt. This is your last opportunity to make sure the corners of your quilt are square and the edges are straight.

Use a ruler to create new, straight edges for your quilt by measuring from a straight element in the quilt, such as a seam between blocks, a sashing line, or an interior border. Lay your ruler on one end of the quilt and make a chalk mark where you want to trim the edge. Move the opposite end of the quilt, measure the same distance, and make a second mark. A chalk-line reel makes it easy to mark the entire length of the quilt edge. Pin the chalk line to the quilt on the marks you made and snap the chalk line to give you a clear guideline for trimming the edge. Sometimes it helps to have someone help you snap the line so you can keep the edge of the quilt secure and the line taut. *Photo 3–16*

Measuring the Quilt

After you have trimmed the quilt, you can check the edges, one against the other, by folding both sides of the quilt to the center (described in more detail on page 5). This measures both edges against the middle.

Are they all they same? If so, record that measurement. If the edges and the center do not measure the same, you need to check the corners to make sure they are 90 degrees. If the quilt edges are not straight or the corners are not 90 degrees before you add the binding, they certainly won't be after you stitch the binding onto the quilt.

Sewing the Binding

Using double-fold French binding as an example, make the binding from bias strips cut 2¼" wide. This makes a binding ⅜" wide, which is suitable for most quilted projects. Sew enough strips together, end to end, to fit the perimeter of the quilt plus at least 12". Cut a 45-degree angle on one end.

Fold the strip in half lengthwise, wrong sides together, and press without stretching the fabric. Lay the raw edge of the binding along the raw edge of the quilt top, starting about 6" to 8" from a corner.

For a smooth finish, use your sewing machine to sew the binding to the quilt top. Leave at least 6" unsewn at the beginning to aid in joining the ends after the binding has been stitched around the entire quilt.

At the corner, measure and place a pin ¼" from the next edge of the quilt top. Begin sewing with a scant ¼" seam allowance. Sew until you reach the pin then take a couple of backstitches to secure the threads. *Photo 3–17*

Raise the presser foot and cut the threads. Fold the binding up to form a 45-degree angle in the corner. *Photo 3–18*

Next, fold the binding down along the second edge, making sure the fold is even with the edge of the quilt at the corner. *Photo 3–19*

Measure and place a pin ¼" from the second corner. Begin sewing at the folded edge at the corner and continue until you come to the next pin. Backstitch and cut the threads.

Sew the binding on the third side in the same manner. On the fourth side, start stitching from the corner and stop about 6" from where you started to leave room to join the ends. Backstitch as before and cut the threads.

Joining the Ends
You can join the ends of the binding in two different ways. Option 1 explains how to join the ends when you cut a miter at the beginning of the binding strip. Option 2 shows how to use a straight cut for both the beginning and ending of the binding strip.

Option 1. To join the ends with a mitered seam, cut the beginning end of the strip at a 45-degree angle. Working on a flat surface of sufficient size, open the beginning miter out flat so you can see which direction the miter goes.

Open the tail end and place the beginning end on top of it. Make sure that both ends are lying smooth and flat. Using the beginning end as a guide, use a pencil and ruler to mark the miter on the tail end. *Photo 3–20*

Move the beginning end aside. Place your ruler on the marked miter on the tail end and mark another line ½" away from the first line, toward the beginning end. This ½" is for the seam allowances that are needed for both ends. *Photo 3–21*

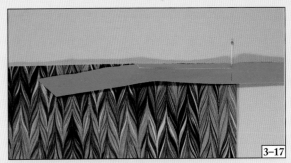
Sew binding to edge, stopping ¼" from corner.

Form a 45-degree angle in the corner.

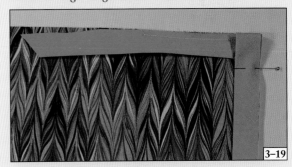
Fold binding down along the second edge.

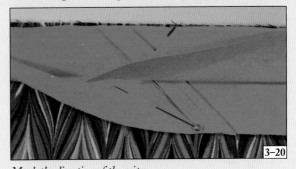
Mark the direction of the miter.

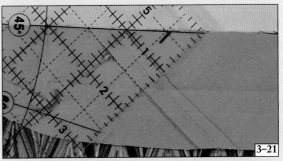
Measure ½" from the first mark for seam allowances.

Match ends, right sides together.

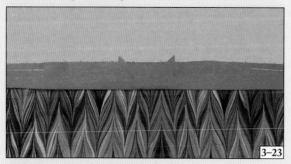

Finger press seam and refold binding.

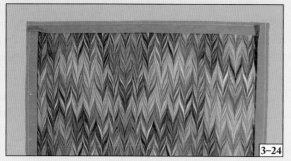

Stitch the remaining section to the quilt.

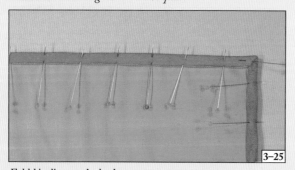

Fold binding to the back.

Finger press a 45-degree angle on the beginning end.

Cut off the excess binding on the second drawn line. Pin the two miters, right sides together, allowing the edges to extend ¼" on both sides. *Photo 3–22*

With the binding opened flat, stitch the two mitered ends together and finger press the seam allowances open. Fold the binding in half again and stitch the remaining section to the quilt. This method gives a very neat finish to your binding. *Photos 3–23 & 3–24*

Fold the binding over the back of the quilt and blindstitch it in place by hand using stitches spaced close together. The stitches should be spaced as close as they would be if sewn by machine to make a well-applied, secure binding. *Photo 3–25*

Make sure the machine stitching line is covered. Also remember to sew the mitered corners closed on both the front and back of the quilt.

Option 2. Cut the beginning of the binding strip with a straight cut. Fold the binding in half, wrong sides together and proceed to stitch the binding to the quilt, leaving an 8" tail at the beginning.

Sew the binding to the quilt, making miters at the corners as shown in Option 1, page 43, photos 3–17 to 3–19.

Open out the fabric on both ends. Fold a 45-degree angle on the beginning end. Finger press the angle. Lay the two strips, right sides up, aligning the raw edges. Now unfold the angle, forming a 90-degree angle with the tail end. *Photo 3–26*

Helpline
Calculating Bias Strips

When cutting bias strips, the length of a bias strip will be 1.414 times the length of the fabric. For example, if your fabric is 18" long (measure along the selvage), a strip cut on the bias (45-degree angle) will be 18" x 1.414. = 25.4". You can use this number to help calculate the number of strips you need to cut to go around the edges of your quilt.

The 45-degree angle you finger pressed is your stitching line. Sew the ends together on the fold line. Check the miter before trimming. *Photo 3–27*

Trim, leaving ¼" seam allowance. Finger press the seam open. Trim ¼" from the seam line and press seam open. Refold the binding and stitch to the quilt. *Photo 3–28*

Fold the binding over the back of the quilt and blindstitch it in place by hand. Make sure the machine-stitching line is covered by the binding. Sew the mitered corners closed on both the front and back of the quilt.

Squared-Corner Binding

You do not need to always make miters on the corners of your binding. It is important to be consistent in the elements of the quilt. If the borders are mitered, a mitered binding will continue that design element better than a binding that has been squared at the corners. If a block has been set into the corner of the border, using a squared corner in the binding would keep the corners consistent.

To stitch the squared corner binding, attach strips of binding to the front top and bottom edges. Trim the ends to form square corners. Fold the binding to the back and blindstitch it in place. *Photo 3–29*

Sew binding to the sides of the quilt, leaving ¼" beyond the corners. Fold in the ¼", making sure the corner is still square. *Photo 3–30*

Stitch on the fold line.

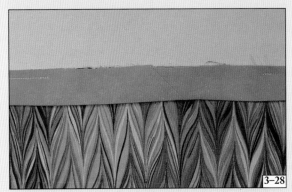

Refold the binding and stitch to the quilt.

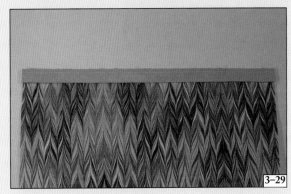

Blindstitch binding on the quilt back.

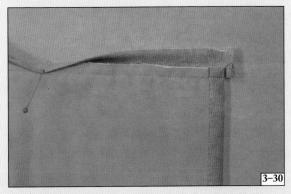

Sew binding to the sides and trim the end, leaving ¼" beyond the corner.

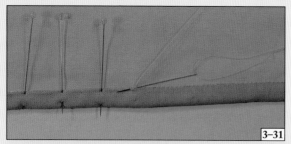

Wrap binding to the back and blindstitch.

3–31

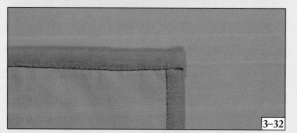

Stitch binding corners closed.

3–32

Wrap the binding to the back and blindstitch in place. Be sure to stitch the folded binding ends closed to help make the binding more secure. *Photos 3–31 & 3–32*

Binding Irregular Edges

Quilts with irregular edges, like Grandmother's Flower Garden or Double Wedding Ring, may be finished in a variety of ways. They can be bound with binding. (Remember that any curves will require a bias binding to fold around the curve properly.) Another option is to fold in the edges of both the front and back and blindstitch the edge; this technique does not protect the edges for wear like a binding can. A separate facing can be made from a strip of fabric and laid right sides together onto the quilt top. Stitch along the irregular edge using the edge of the quilt as a guide, clip along curves and indentations, turn, and whip in place on the back of the quilt. *Photo 3–33*

Hong Kong Edge

The Hong Kong edge finish is traditionally used to encase seam allowances on garments with a lightweight fabric, like tricot binding or bias tape. It is used because it is neat and attractive.

You can use a variation of the Hong Kong finishing technique to bind the edge of a quilt. Cut a 2" wide bias strip of fabric for the binding to fit the perimeter of the quilt. Sew the right side of the binding to the back side of the quilt with a ½" seam allowance. The corners are stitched like traditional French binding (see page 42) except you are using a single layer of fabric. *Photo 3–34*

Fold the binding over the edge to the front of the quilt. You will have a raw edge on the front. Stitch ¼" away from the previous stitching (¾" from the edge of the quilt). This stitching will hold the binding securely while you apply a decorative bias strip over the raw edge. *Photo 3–35*

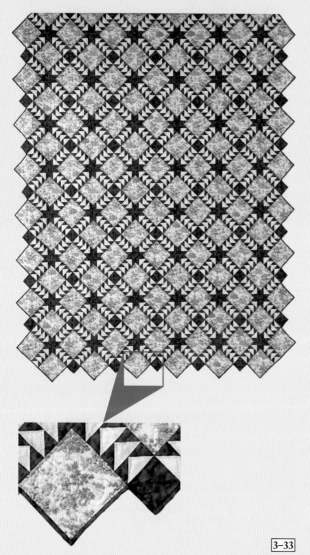

WILD GOOSE CHASE by Klonda Holt, Kansas City, Missouri

3–33

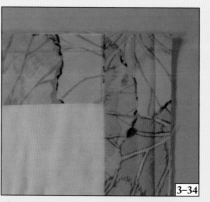

Sew a bias strip to the back of the quilt.

3–34

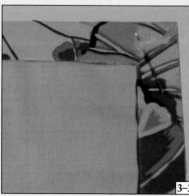

Fold binding to the front and stitch ¾" from edg

3–3

Cut a ¾" wide contrasting bias strip of fabric to make into a single-fold strip to cover the raw edge of the binding. Align the raw edge of the bias strip with the raw edge of the binding, right sides together, on the quilt front, folding the corners using the method for French binding on page 42. Sew using a scant ¼" seam allowance. To join the ends, fold the edge under ¼" and overlap the ends. Carefully fold and press the bias strip into thirds, making sure the raw edge of the binding is covered. *Photo 3–36*

Stitch down the folded edge of the bias strip, using one of these stitches: straight stitch, narrow zigzag, blind hem, or a decorative stitch. If you prefer hand stitching, use a hand blindstitch to secure the folded edge of the bias strip.

Novelty Edge Treatments

If you are making fun quilts, like those that use chenille techniques or the raw-edge rag techniques, you might want to use an edge treatment that fits with the style of the quilt. When it seems appropriate, try using fuzzy raw edges, fluffy binding, or scalloped fused binding.

Fuzzy Raw Edges

No binding is needed for this technique. After you have trimmed the edges of your quilt, stitch to ¾" from the edge on all sides. Make cuts every ½" through all layers (top, batting, and backing) around the perimeter of the quilt, making sure you don't cut through the stitches. Fluff the edges using a wire or a chenille brush. Spray the edges with water as you brush to help with the fluffing. Washing the quilt will help make the edges fluffier. *Photo 3–37*

Fluffy Binding

Add a binding with a fluffy inner edge all at once. Cut bias strips of fabric 2¼" wide by the length of each side of the quilt. Stitch the bias strips to the wrong side of the quilt. The strips will overlap at the corners.

Once the binding strips are attached on all four sides of the quilt, press the binding strips out flat. *Photo 3–38*

Fold the binding over the edge to the front of the quilt and stitch ½" from the edge. You should have ¾" extending beyond your stitched line toward the center of the quilt. *Photo 3–39*

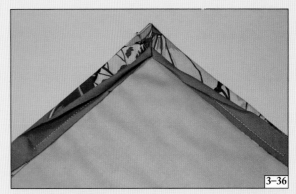
Stitch on the fold line.

Fuzzy raw edges should be fluffed with a brush.

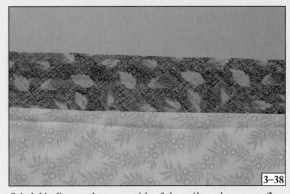
Stitch binding to the wrong side of the quilt and press out flat.

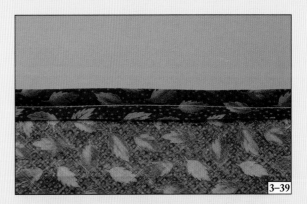
Fold binding to front and stitch ½" from folded edge.

Clip the raw edge and fluff.

Threads are couched on a quilted edge.

Pink the binding edges and fold the wrong sides together.

Clip the raw edge of the binding ½" apart. Fluff the edges using a wire or a chenille brush. Spray the edges with water as you brush to help with the fluffing. Washing the quilt will help make the edges fluffier. *Photo 3–40*

Couched Cord or Yarn Edge

Use some of those decorative stitches on your sewing machine to couch one or more cords or yarns to the edge of a quilt. Matching or contrasting threads can be used, depending on whether you want the stitching to show. Have fun with this technique and twist a variety of cords or heavy threads together using colors from the quilt to carry them to the very edge of your piece. *Photo 3–41*

Raw-Edge Fused Binding

Sometimes an easy novelty edge for a wallhanging might be appropriate. Press fusible web to the wrong side of strips of fabric to fit the edges of your quilt. Keep the paper backing on the fusible. The width of the strips should be two times the desired width of the binding plus ½" for trimming.

Use pinking shears or a pinking or wavy blade in your rotary cutter to cut a decorative design along both long edges of each strip. With the fusible paper backing still intact, fold the binding with wrong sides together to crease the center of the binding. *Photo 3–42*

Remove the paper backing from the fusible. Insert the raw edge of the quilt into the fold of the binding. Carefully press the binding in place, making sure the raw edge is pushed into the fold of the binding as you go. *Photo 3–43*

If you wish to miter the corners, keep the top and bottom binding sections straight, and miter both ends of the side borders. This will give you the look of mitered corners without having to worry about meeting two miters exactly in the corners. *Photo 3–44*

Remove paper from fusible and insert raw edge of quilt into fold.

Miter the binding on the sides.

Variation: Use straight edges on the binding, fuse them in place, and finish the edges with decorative stitches.

This is a fun technique to use on some of those quilts that will not be laundered. If you are making fabric postcards or artist trading cards, try this fused technique for adding a decorative binding.

Heavy Metal Edge

Some quilts call for an edge that carries out a theme. In MR. GOODWRENCH MEETS THE RUBBER BAND MAN, Lois Arnold inserted a metal jacket zipper to finish the edges of her quilt. The zipper emphasizes the tool man, which was a photo image printed on fabric. What a fun, creative way to blend the quilt with a special edge treatment. *Photo 3–45*

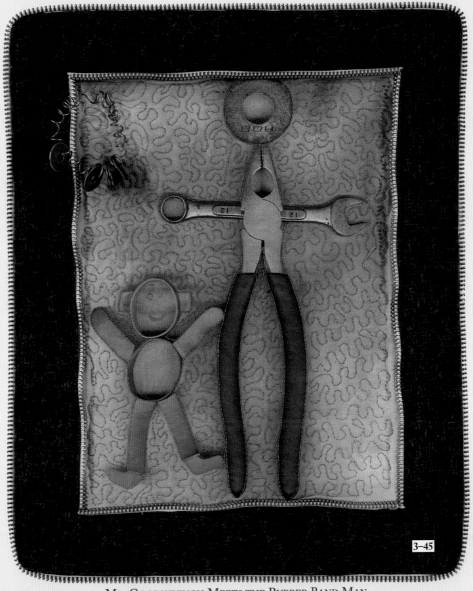

3–45

MR. GOODWRENCH MEETS THE RUBBER BAND MAN,
by Lois Embree Arnold, Montgomery, Alabama

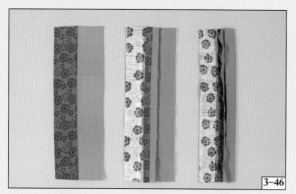

Sew the strips together along the length of the strips.

Sew the binding to the front of the quilt.

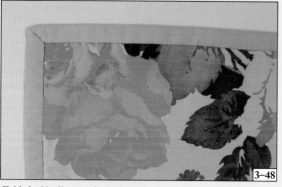

Fold the binding to the back of the quilt and blindstitch.

Complete two-sided binding

Two-sided Binding

There may be quilts that are reversible and you want a different color for the binding on each side. Cut strips of two fabrics. The width of the strips will be the desired width of the binding plus seam allowances, i.e., a ½" finished binding will require 1¼" strips (½" finished binding + ¼" for joint seam allowance + ½" for seam to apply binding to quilt.)

Sew the strips together along the length of the strips using ¼" seam allowance. Pressing the seam open makes it easier to roll the edge after stitching to the quilt. *Photo 3–46*

Using a single layer of fabric and ½" seam allowance, sew the binding to the front of the quilt. Double check to make sure you have the desired binding fabric for the front of the quilt. Use the instructions for turning the corner of the binding on page 43. *Photo 3–47*

This wider seam allowance will make your binding full to the edge with batting. Fold the binding to the back of the quilt. Turn under ½" to just cover the stitching line and blindstitch the turned edge. *Photos 3–48 & 3–49*

Label Your Quilt

Once you have completed the binding, you are ready to put a label with your name, city, state, date, and any other information you wish, on the back of your quilt. If the quilt is being given for a special occasion, include that information on the label. Make your label using a permanent marker, hand or machine embroidery, or machine stitches for the lettering.

Keep Your Sense of Humor

If you've ever been frustrated when your stitching didn't turn out exactly the way it looks in a book, you'll identify with the quilter in the story on page 51, by A. B. Silver. I happened upon "Bind for Glory" on the Internet, and the author graciously gave permission to include it in this book. I hope you get the same chuckle from it that I did. Does it sound like anything you have experienced?

BIND FOR GLORY

"No, no, no," she yelled at the book she was reading. She was standing over the large ironing board in her sewing room, the book on one side, the strips of binding she was making for the new quilt on the other.

"You can't take that away from me," I finished, but from her tone and the frown on her face, I knew she wasn't singing some old song. She was upset and frustrated. "You upset?" I asked.

"I did the binding wrong, " she said.

"How wrong?" I asked. I had become used to her saying she had done something wrong in her efforts to complete five hundred quilts in ten days, or so it seemed. I hadn't seen her much since Christmas passed. She came out of her sewing room only on rare occasions, and lately that was to exclaim that another quilt was finished. And she was never satisfied. Something was always wrong, she complained. A crooked square, a wavy sashing (I told her to wave back), a border that was off by a thousandth of an inch, a six-pointed star that only had five and a half points. "Looks good to me," I always said.

"I followed the new instructions in this book," she said, holding a strip of blue fabric up to my face. "Just look at how this binding looks."

I looked at a blue blur as she passed it quickly in front of my eyes. "Looks fine to me," I said. I wasn't just being nice. It was a fine blur.

"I know it's fine. It's almost perfect, but it's not what the book says it should look like. "

"Get another book," I said. And that, of course, was the real problem. She had too many quilting books.

"But this is the new one I got for my birthday," she said, dropping the strip of fabric and lifting the book up to my face. "Four Billion and Eight Ways to Create the Perfect Binding," the book title read.

"So, which one did you use?" I asked.

"I did Binding Number Forty-three. It says to cut the fabric on the bias and turn it toward the sunny side of the house and iron it with a cold iron while stretching it to the left," she said.

Did you stand on one foot?" I asked. Sometimes quilting directions are a bit odd. But she always told me the Quilter's Creed was, "Anything that works."

"Don't be silly," she said.

"I'm silly?" I asked. "I didn't turn the fabric to the sunny side of the house during the foggiest day of winter."

"You know I'm making that up. The instructions are clear and useful and easy to follow."

"So why are you yelling, 'No, no, no,' and frowning?" I asked.

"Because the book doesn't agree with my other books," she said, and she dropped the large book to the ironing board, right on top of the blue binding.

"So it's a book war?" I asked.

"It's a directions war," she said.

"You're having problems with the directions again?" I knew she had screamed early in her quilting life when she had followed the directions to cut out fabric to make a quilt only to find out after all the fabric was cut out that the measurements in the book or magazine were wrong. After the second time she had done that, she had learned to make only one square before she built the largest scrap heap in Quiltland from wrongly cut or wrongly sewn or wrongly batted or wrongly quilted fabric.

"I'm having trouble because I learned how to make binding a good way, and then I read directions for a new better technique for making binding, and then I read directions for a superior way to make binding, and then I read an article on eight hundred ways to avoid making bad binding, and then I read another article in a quilting magazine on how to make simple binding in an easy way, and the binding holding my head together is getting frayed." She said that all in one breath. Quilters can do that.

"Why don't you just go with what works," I suggested helpfully.

"They all work," she said, "but then an article in the latest issue of 'Quilting Made Darn Easy' or the newest book called, 'Cooking, Cleaning, and Making Binding in Your Spare Time,' comes along, and all the books say there's a new miracle technique for me to bind my way into heaven."

"How many quilts have you made so far?" I asked.

"A couple," she said, underestimating the truth by about a dozen, maybe two dozen. Lately, she's become a quilt factory.

"And they all have binding?"

"Of course."

"And you did the binding?"

"Who else lives in this house who has a terminal addiction to stash and stitches?" she asked.

"And all the binding fits the quilts you made?"

"Yes," she said, looking at me now, her attention undivided, which was rare, as ninety percent of her attention the past year was always on some aspect of quilting.

"And you've made mock binding, and straight binding and bias binding with mitered corners and diagonal seams and French kisses?"

"That's French binding," she said. She was paying attention.

"And lapped binding and single-fold and double-fold and scalloped?"

"Do you know what you're talking about?" she asked.

"No, but sometimes you read out loud, and I pick up things."

"How about picking up the telephone and ordering me some more fabric so I can make more binding," she said. It wasn't a question. It wasn't a request. It was a quilter's command.

"What kind of binding?" I asked.

"I don't know yet. I'll see what the new book says."

"New book?"

"The one you're going to order for me."

"What book am I ordering for you?"

"Dream Binding and Butter Churning Your Way into the New Year," she said.

Why not?

Border Patterns

The patterns for the quilt borders do not have seam allowances. The full-sized patterns can be traced on the seam line and the ¼" seam allowance can be added for pieced designs, and slightly less than ¼" for appliquéd designs.

For appliqué, trace the patterns onto template plastic. Cut them out with very sharp scissors, making the edges as smooth as possible. To transfer the designs onto your fabric, you can use a variety of techniques, such as drawing around the templates directly onto the right side of the fabric or drawing the designs onto freezer paper and pressing the freezer paper onto the fabric.

Use your favorite techniques for appliquéing or piecing. The author prefers using freezer paper pressed to the wrong side of the fabric (remember to reverse the patterns for this technique) with needle-turn appliqué and uses a master pattern drawn on clear vinyl for placing the appliqué pieces.

Vinyl Overlay for Appliqué

Trace appliqué designs with a permanent marker on clear heavyweight decorator vinyl. You'll find clear vinyl in fabric shops and the fabric sections of department stores. It comes in a variety of thicknesses. The heaviest weight will have less stretch and be more accurate.

Pin the top edge of the vinyl to the top edge of the background fabric. Slide the appliqué pieces into position by raising the bottom edge of the vinyl. Position the appliqué piece and pin it in place. Continue laying appliqué pieces on the background until you have placed as many pieces as you want to work on at one time. On some designs, you will need to appliqué the base pieces, re-pin the vinyl to the top edge of the fabric, and position the next layer to the background.

Copyright Guidelines

There is often confusion about when you should give credit for using designs from books, patterns, other artwork, or other copyrighted sources. If you use a pattern or another artwork, you really are making a derivative work, even if the medium is totally different. It doesn't make any difference how many different pattern sources are used, your quilt will be a derivative work of all of them.

The copyright laws give the copyright holder the right to control who may use the likeness of their artwork, including derivative work.

The author of this book grants you, the purchaser of this book, the right to photocopy the designs to use in your personal quilts and other artwork projects. Quilts made from these patterns may be entered and displayed in quilt and art shows, provided the author and quiltmaker (if different from the author) are given credit for the design.

If you use other sources, you will want to check to see what the policy is for entering shows, especially for those shows with monetary awards. Authors and publishers all have their own policies regarding the use of the patterns from their books. To avoid copyright problems, it's always wise to ask before you use designs for anything that involves money.

The Glistening Rose Garden

Diamond Pieced Border and Quilted Feather Border

By Judy Laquidara, Owensboro, Kentucky. Quilt size: 72" x 88". Pieced border: 4" wide. Quilted border: 8" wide.

Technique: Pieced Diamond Border & Feathered Quilting Design

This pieced border is created by using an isosceles triangle shape in the center. Paper piecing will aid in getting perfect points and help control the bias edge you will be stitching.

It is recommended that you add solid strips as borders on each side of the pieced border. There are several reasons for adding these solid border strips:

- They stabilize the edge of the quilt before the pieced borders are added.
- The strips lessen the bulk because the seams in the borders do not meet seams in the quilt top.
- The strips can be used as a "fudge factor." If your quilt does not equal a measurement that can be divided equally for the pieced blocks, add strips to increase the size.

Example: Your quilt measures 45" x 45" (finished). If the finished size of the quilt were 48" x 48", the edge could easily be divided into convenient block sizes (divisible by 2 for a 24" block, 4 for a 12" block, or 6 for an 8" block). So we need to add 3" to the 45" quilt to make it 48".

You will be adding borders to both sides of the quilt, so divide the 3" by 2, which makes each finished border width 1½". Add ¼" seam allowances and cut the borders 2" wide by the measured length of the quilt edge.

Add these borders to two opposite sides of the quilt. Press. Measure the length for the other two sides of the quilt and add these to the quilt.

After adding the solid borders, you can make your paper-piecing template for the pieced border. The 48" finished size of the quilt edge can be divided equally by 4 (48 ÷ 4 = 12 blocks).

This design is made up of two blocks to create one diamond. In our 48" quilt, you will have six diamonds (48 ÷ 8 = 6 repeats).

Draw two 4" squares. Place a mark at the midpoint of the outer edge of each square. Draw lines from these midpoints to the opposite corners, creating an isosceles triangle in each square. This is your border unit. Fig. 1

Fig. 1

For paper piecing, you will need one paper pattern for each unit in your border.

For traditional piecing, make a template for the entire isosceles triangle and one for the half triangle shape.

Join the block units to create the borders for two opposite sides. Fig. 2

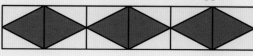

Fig. 2

Sew these borders to the sides of the quilt.

Join the block units for the top and bottom. You will need four squares the same width as the border for the corner. Join the corner squares to each end of your top and bottom borders. Fig. 3

Fig. 3

Add top and bottom pieced borders to the quilt. Add any additional borders. Judy added another narrow border the same size as the inner solid border. The final border is 8" wide to show off a beautiful feather quilting design. See pages 55–57 for the feathered swag and feathered corner quilting patterns. Notice how the background quilting makes the feather quilting design stand out.

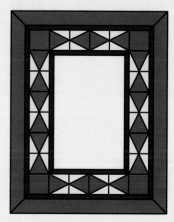

Layout Variations

About Judy Laquidara

In the early 1980s, while living in Lake Charles, Louisiana, Judy was wasting time during her lunch hour and stumbled across a little quilt shop. That little shop consumed many of her lunch hours and her earnings, too!

After moving to Owensboro, Kentucky, Judy purchased a longarm sewing machine, and the rest, as they say, is history. She began perfecting her quilting skills and making quilts, and winning awards, including Best of Contest at the AQS Quilt Exposition, Nashville, Tennessee. Today she teaches piecing and longarm quilting for guilds and conferences.

8" Feathered Corner
quilting pattern

*8" Feathered Swag
quilting pattern*

connect here

connect here

Crazy Patch Border

Blocks by Milford Valley Quilt Guild, Milford, Pennsylvania. Collection of the author.
Quilt size: 45" x 54". Crazy Patch border, 3½" wide.

Technique: Crazy Patch Border

When you have a variety of quilt blocks, as in this group quilt made by the Milford Valley Quilt Guild, Milford, Pennsylvania, making a crazy patch lets you combine many different fabrics to create the border.

Supplies

Fabrics: Use scraps of fabrics from the blocks in the quilt top or add other fabrics that are similar. Because this is a foundation-pieced pattern, you can use the colors in random order or choose to repeat the colors in a controlled pattern, i.e., red, blue, red, blue, etc.

Thread: Use a neutral-colored thread. A medium gray works well with medium to dark fabric colors, or use a medium taupe or tan for light to medium fabrics.

Cutting tools: A rotary cutter, mat, and ruler will be helpful for trimming the fabric as you foundation piece.

Foundation patterns: Make enough foundation patterns to fit the perimeter of your quilt. You can photocopy or scan and print the patterns. The author prefers to use vellum paper because the lines can be seen from both sides. You can use any thin paper, from inexpensive typing paper to tracing paper.

Two patterns are provided. One block measures 3½" x 6", and the other block measures 3½" x 8". To adjust the border to a width narrower than 3½", simply cut the pattern to the width desired.

Foundation Piecing

Foundation piecing is as simple as sewing on the line. You can use one of the blocks, repeating it along the length of the border, or alternate the two blocks to make the border. You can also turn the blocks 180 degrees to add even more variety.

Some people think that foundation piecing is a quick method of sewing. It is not a quick method. Instead, it is a way to achieve accuracy, and that is especially helpful when several people are sewing the blocks. If you are planning a special color scheme, you can mark the colors on the foundation patterns to aid you when you are sewing.

The fabrics you have will determine how you sew them for your quilt. For example, if your strips are not wide enough to cover a

section of the block, just sew the strip in place and add another fabric to complete that section. No one will know that it was supposed to be one fabric covering that area except you, and you aren't going to tell.

The numbers on the block are the stitching order for adding the strips. You will sew from the right side of the paper foundation (you can read the number right side up from this side). The fabric will be placed on the opposite side (the numbers will be backward).

Begin by trimming the length of your first fabric strip, making sure it extends at least ¼" beyond the edges of the pattern. Then place the strip, with the wrong side against the paper pattern, covering section 1. Place a pin to hold the strip in place.

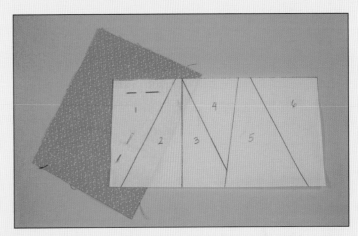

Fold the pattern on the line joining sections 1 and 2. Trim the fabric, leaving a ¼" seam allowance. You will find that by trimming before you sew makes it much easier to position the next strip.

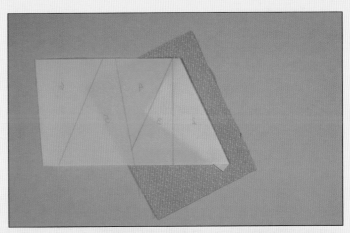

Align fabric 2 along the piece you just trimmed. Again, make sure the fabric extends beyond the edges of the pattern. Shorten the stitch length on your sewing machine to 15 stitches per inch. This shortened stitch will compensate for the removal of the paper foundation and hold the fabrics securely together. Fold out the pattern to cover the seam allowance so you can read the numbers on the pattern. Begin sewing one stitch before the line and end one stitch beyond the line.

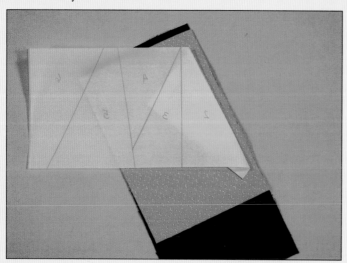

Remember this sequence for foundation piecing:

Fold the pattern back.

Trim the fabric.

Position the strip.

Fold the pattern out.

Sew on the line.

Press the fabric.

Cut off the ends of the strip.

Continue adding fabrics, following the stitching sequence. Before adding each strip, fold the pattern back and trim the seam

allowance to make aligning the next strip easier.

After the pattern is covered, trim the edges adding ¼" seam allowance on all edges.

Join the pattern sections to fit the edge of the quilt by stitching on the outside line of each pattern piece. Sew the borders to the top and bottom, then sew the side borders to the quilt.

Helpline

Keeping Your Place

To keep track of where you have just sewn, place a pin in the last piece stitched. You can check that number to see where you sew next.

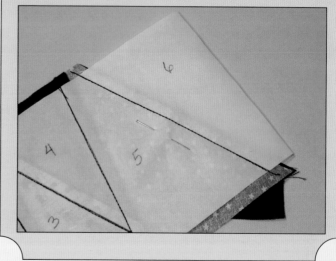

About the Milford Valley Quilt Guild

LONG MAY SHE WAVE – OVER LAND, OVER SEA blocks were made by the Milford Valley quilt guild; assembled by Jean Hoff and Barbar Demczak; quilted by Jean Hoff, Barbara Demczak, Pat Messineo, and Jeanne Sullivan. The guild made this quilt in response to the challenge by the American Quilter's Society to make quilts for raising funds following the September 11, 2001, tragedy in New York. This quilt is now in the collection of the author, who won the bid for it on the eBay auction of these quilts. The Milford Valley Quilters also embroidered blocks of all the presidents and combined them with other 9/11 blocks to make a quilt for President and Mrs. Bush.

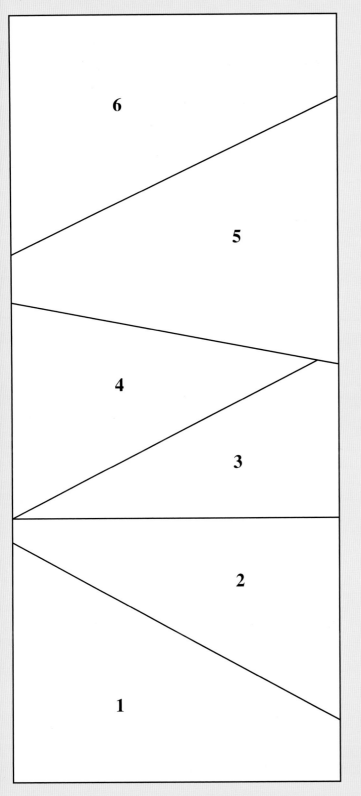

3½" x 8" foundation

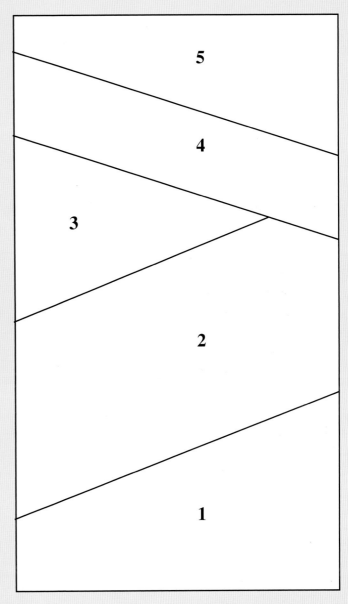

3½" x 6" foundation

Whacky Nine-Patches

By the author. Quilt size: 53" x 67". Block size: 5". Inner border: 1½".

Top & Bottom Checkerboard Four-Patch border: 5½". Side Four-Patch on point borders: 4".

Borders & Finishing Touches 2 – Bonnie K. Browning

The Nine-Patch block is often used in quilts. After participating in a 12½" Nine-Patch block exchange with the online Fairie Goddess Mothers quilting group, the author decided to create a quilt with a very different look. The blocks were whacked both vertically and horizontally, and half-squares were stitched to each quadrant of the block. Two styles of Four-Patch borders were added to complete the quilt.

Technique: Nine-Patch Blocks
Twenty 12½" Nine-Patch blocks are needed. You need a total of 1⅛ yards, each of light and dark fabrics, and 2¼ yards of fabric for the half-squares.

Cut 4½" strips of light and dark scrap fabrics to make the blocks. Sew the strips into strip-sets. Rows 1 and 3 are Dark/Light/Dark. Row 2 is Light/Dark/Light. Stitch 20 blocks.

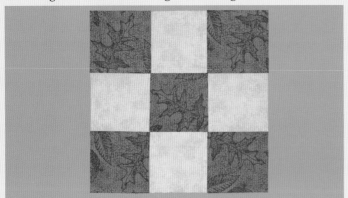

Whacking the Blocks
Cut the Nine-Patches into fourths, by cutting them in half both vertically and horizontally.

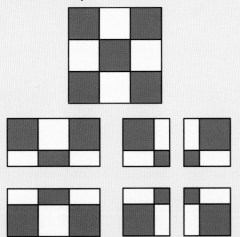

Trim the quadrants to 6" to make sure all of the squares are the same size. This is especially important if you have exchanged blocks where seam allowances may vary.

Cut 6" squares to make half-squares. Draw a diagonal line on the plain square. Layer one 6" square over the pieced blocks.

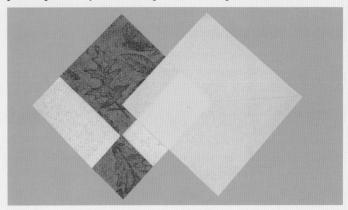

Stitch ¼" on both sides of the diagonal line. Cut apart on the drawn line. Now you have two different blocks.

Lay out the blocks following the quilt photo on page 62, or have fun with the blocks and make your own layout. You can use any layout that would be suitable for a Log Cabin quilt.

Four-Patch Border

The Four-Patch is used in many quilt blocks. The Four-Patch can also be used for sashing strips and borders, with the units set next to each other (in a checkerboard fashion) or on the diagonal (on-point).

To determine the size of block to fit the edge of your quilt, use the paper-folding method in Making Borders Fit on page 5. See the table on page 65 for cutting instructions for Four-Patch blocks in different sizes.

To make a border, you can use two (light and dark) or three fabrics (light, medium, and dark). The Four-Patches can also be made from scraps. Using color placement and setting the blocks on-point will lead the eye across or around your quilt. Make a simple checkerboard-style border by joining Four-Patch blocks together to fit the perimeter of the quilt.

Create a sawtooth look to that Four-Patch border by adding a light strip to one side and a dark strip to the opposite side.

For the on-point setting, you will need to sew a triangle to each corner of the Four-Patch. Unify a scrap border with one fabric or one color for all the triangles. It is an easy border to sew.

Sewing a Four-Patch Unit

Use a light and a dark or medium fabric for each Four-Patch unit. High contrast between the two fabrics lets you use these units as a design element in your quilt.

Example: To make a border that finishes 3" wide, sew a 2" strip of the light fabric, right sides together with a 2" dark or medium strip. Press the seam allowances toward the darker fabric. Cut this pieced strip into 2" segments.

To finish the Four-Patch units, lay out the segments as shown. Reverse one segment so the dark squares are in opposite corners, and sew the segments together with a ¼" seam allowance.

Four-Patches with Triangles

To make the border unit shown in the following figure, add triangles to your Four-Patches. To make the triangles, cut a strip 3" wide of a medium fabric and cut it into 3" squares. **[3" Four Patch ÷ 1.414 = 2.1216" + ⅞" = 2.996"]** Cut the squares diagonally into triangles. Four triangles (two squares) are required for each Four-Patch. Sew a triangle to each side of the Four-Patch. Take care not to stretch the bias edge of the triangle as you sew. The resulting border will finish 4¼" wide.

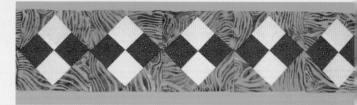

Sewing Four-Patch Borders to Quilt

Two different borders were made for Whacky Nine-Patches. For the top and bottom borders, Four-Patch blocks were sewn together to fit the width of the quilt. A light 1½" strip will be sewn to one side, and a dark 1½" strip will be added to the opposite side. Align the raw edges and sew, using ¼" seam allowances.

The Four-Patch blocks with triangles added are sewn to the sides of the quilt. If your strip is not quite long enough to fit the edge of your quilt, cut squares larger than the block, i.e., 5" for a 3" block, and cut them into triangles. Sew these larger triangles to the top and bottom Four-Patches in this border to extend the border.

Cutting Four-Patches

Border Width (finished)	Four-Patch (cut strips & segments)
3"	2"
3½"	2¼"
4"	2 ½"
4½"	2¾"
5"	3"

Helpline

Aligning Seams

To align the center seams, with right sides together, push the seams together until they meet. Once you've sewn a few of these units together, you will be able to do it without using any pins. Butting the two seam allowances like this will make a good join once they are sewn.

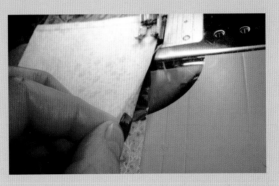

Cutting Triangles

Some of the squares are slightly oversized for ease in cutting. If necessary, trim the finished units, leaving ¼" seam allowances beyond the points.

Cutting Triangles

Four-Patch Size (finished)	Cut Squares (cut in half diagonally)	Approx. Border Width (finished)
3"	3"	4¼"
3½"	3⅜"	5"
4"	3¾"	5⅝"
4½"	4⅛"	6⅜"
5"	4½"	7"

Layout Diagram

Windmill – Twisted Log Cabin

Quilt Pattern with Pieced Border

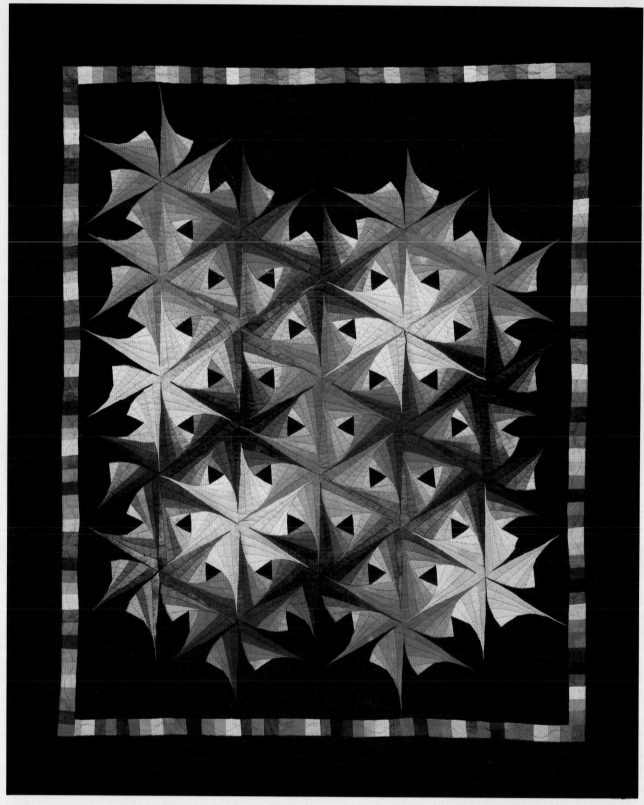

By Susan Rice, Powder Springs, Georgia. Quilt size: 60" x 72". 8" equilateral triangle.

Quilt Pattern: Due to popular demand, the entire pattern for the WINDMILL – TWISTED LOG CABIN is provided to make a 35¾" x 40" quilt.

Technique: Foundation-pieced blocks with pieced border

Many quilters have requested the complete pattern for the WINDMILL – TWISTED LOG CABIN quilt. The author shared the paper-piecing technique for this triangle-shaped Log Cabin block on *Simply Quilts* (HGTV). This design was originally pictured in *Log Cabin with a Twist* by Barbara Kaempfer (AQS, 1995), where you will find instructions for drawing twisted Log Cabin designs in squares, diamonds, and other shapes.

The equilateral triangle block is 8" on each side. Rather than cutting individual pieces for each triangle shape inside the block, you will be cutting 1⅜" strips, which is large enough to fit the widest log. The log seam allowances will be trimmed to ¼" as each seam is sewn.

This pattern looks stunning in hand-dyed fabrics, batiks, solids, or tone-on-tone prints. A variety of color values helps to add dimension to the design. Each triangle block contains a center triangle and three gradated sections. Each section is made from six color values (or three values can be repeated twice). The colors start with very light in the center, grading out to very dark, or you can start with very dark in the center, grading out to very light for a different look.

Read through the instructions before you begin. If you do so, you will see why we you need to make the colored road map to follow for sewing. There are other tips that will help you stitch sew the Windmill—Twisted Log Cabin blocks, as well.

Supplies

Foundations: Note that the foundations do not contain seam allowances. You will need to remember to leave ¼" seam allowances beyond the foundations as you sew. The advantage of this method is that it eliminates the tedious job of tearing the foundations from the seam allowances.

Colored pencils: Use colored pencils to mark the colors on each of the pattern foundations. Do not use crayons because you will be ironing over the patterns, and crayons will melt into your fabric, your iron, or both. Try alternating warm and cool colors, dark against light, to make your windmills stand out.

Sewing machine: Start with a new needle in your machine. Clean the bobbin area and oil your machine before you begin sewing.

Thread: Use a neutral color (gray, taupe, or tan) to blend with your fabrics. Gray will blend with blues and greens; tans will blend with yellows, oranges, and reds. Wind several bobbins before you start sewing so you don't have to stop to do that.

Windmill fabric: Use fat quarters of fabric in six values (very light, light, medium light, medium, dark, and very dark) for each of the eight different windmill colors (total of 48 fat quarters).

There are a couple of other options you can use for choosing fabrics for this quilt your windmills. Try using only three values of each color and repeat each one twice, or use a single fabric for each windmill. All of these options have been successful in my workshops for this quilt.

Background fabric: select a dark color (black, navy, dark green, etc.) 2¼ yards.

Outer border: ⅝ yd.

Backing: 1⅜ yd. (1 panel 40" x at least 43")

Batting: 40" x 44"

Binding: ⅜ yd.

Making the Windmills

Foundations: For your foundations, trace or print 32 copies of the triangle pattern (page 72) on vellum or other lightweight, see-through paper. Make sure you can easily read the patch numbers (1 to 19) on the foundations.

Vellum is the author's choice for the foundations even though it costs more than regular paper, because the lines can be seen through it from either side and it tears away easily.

Some printers can distort the pattern though, so before you print all the foundations, always test one for accuracy, as follows: Measure the foundation triangle to make sure it is still 8" on each side. If you use a photocopy machine, you may find that the pattern grows slightly. If so, try copying the pattern at 99 percent and measure again. Continue reducing the percentage until the foundation triangle measures 8" on each side.

Cut each triangle block on the outside line, which is the seam line for joining the blocks together. Cut four of the foundation triangles in half to use for the outside edges of the quilt.

Road Map: Coloring in each triangle with colored pencils will give you a road map to follow as you sew. Do not skip this step. When you have so many different strips to sew, and because you are sewing the strips Log Cabin-style (going around and around the center), it is very easy to get lost and forget which color you need to sew next. Just pin the triangle foundations to a piece of muslin and hang it on your design wall to complete your road map. Take one triangle foundation at a time to the sewing machine to sew, and then replace it on the road map.

Color the pattern for a road map.

You can make your quilt any size. Simply build your road map to the size you want your quilt to be. You will need a foundation pattern for each triangle in this quilt. Try making a wallhanging or a pillow by making only one windmill with a black or other dark fabric for the background, or a bed-sized quilt with 23 windmills as shown in Susan Rice's quilt shown on page 66. To calculate the size of your quilt, the width of the base of each triangle finishes 8", and the height is 7". The pattern instructions are for a 35¾" x 40" wall quilt made of eight windmills.

Cutting the Fabric

Windmills: Sort the fat quarters into the colors needed for each windmill. Cut the fat quarters into 1⅜" wide strips, which includes ½" for seam allowances plus ⅛" for fudge factor. Cut one to three strips of each fabric for each windmill you are going to make. If you want to repeat a color, you will need to cut six strips.

Background: For the block centers (patch 1), cut two strips 2¼" x 42". Cut the strips into 32 2¼" squares.

For the background, cut one 1⅜" wide strip across the fabric (selvage to selvage) for each block section.

Sewing the Blocks

To make a block, set your sewing machine with a short stitch length (12–15 stitches per inch). Pin a 2¼" square of the background fabric on the center back of the pattern foundation. *The wrong side of the fabric will be next to the pattern for this piece only.* The center of every triangle is the background fabric.

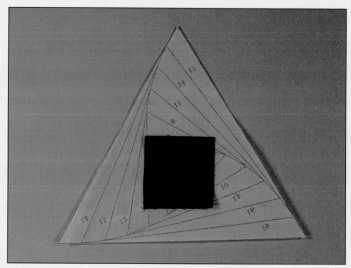

Pin the center in place on the back of the pattern.

Flip the fabric foundation over to see the fabric from the front side. Make sure the seam lines for patch 1 are all covered plus ¼" for seam allowances.

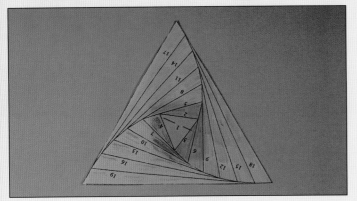

Turn the pattern to the front with the center pinned in place.

On the front side of the pattern (you should be able to read the numbers), fold and finger press the pattern foundation on the line that joins log 2 to the center patch. Lay your ruler with the ¼" line along the folded pattern foundation edge and trim the fabric seam allowance to ¼". Now that the fabric is trimmed, it is easy to align fabric log 2 with the center patch.

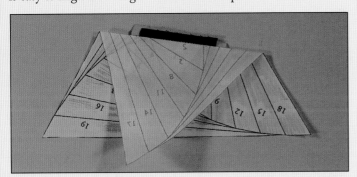

Fold the pattern, trim the center fabric, and line up log 2 with the trimmed edge.

Cut a length of the fabric log 2 strip so it extends at least ½" beyond the seam line you will be sewing. Do not skimp in the length of the fabric strips for the logs. It is much easier to trim off the extra fabric than it is to pick out stitches. "Unsewing" because the strip is too short is not fun. It is more efficient to make the logs slightly longer and trim away any excess.

Pin fabric log 2 in place, *right sides together*, aligning the raw edge with the trimmed edge of the center patch. From the right side of the pattern, *begin sewing at the narrow end of the triangle.* Sew on the line, starting one stitch before the line and ending one stitch beyond the end of the line. Fold the log out and press. Note:

Place a pin in the log you have just sewn to help you keep your place. The pin also holds the log in place as you do your trimming before you sew on log 3. Try it ... you will find that it works!

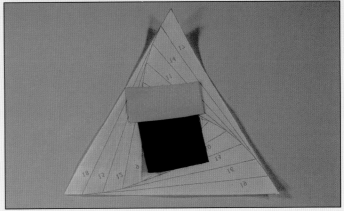

Log 2 is stitched to the foundation.

Repeat sewing additional logs onto the foundation. Continue sewing in the Log Cabin style, around and around. Always remember to fold the pattern back and trim before you sew the next log. As you complete a triangle block, pin it back in place on your road map. Before long, you will be ready to sew a whole row of blocks together.

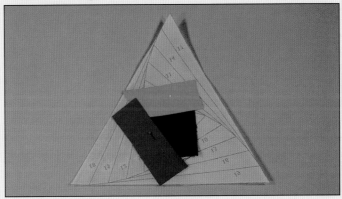

Sew log 3 and mark with a pin.

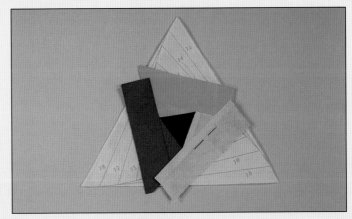

Seven logs are stitched to the foundation.

Keep the foundation paper on the triangles until you have sewn them together. The paper helps to keep the quilt stable because you will have many bias edges being joined together.

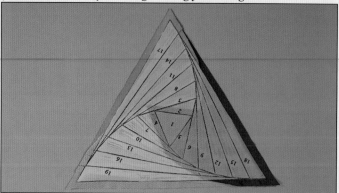

Pattern side of a stitched block

In several triangle blocks, the half triangles are made entirely of the background fabric. You might be tempted to just insert a single triangle there. Don't do that. With all of the seam allowances throughout the pieced triangles, the quilt will never lie flat if you are not consistent in stitching foundation piecing on all of the triangles, including the solid-colored half triangles.

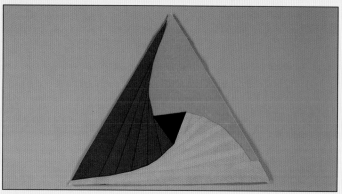

Completed block

Half triangles for edges: To complete the edges, you will need to cut the patterns in half and stitch, following the numbers. (See the layout on page 71.) Re-mark the numbers on some of the logs that have been cut in half. Again, you will stitch around and around in Log Cabin-style for these half triangles, following the numbering.

Joining Blocks

After you have stitched the triangle blocks and repinned them onto your road map, you are ready to sew them together. You will be sewing the triangles blocks in rows; the bases of the triangles will alternate from the top to the bottom. Pin the triangles together by using a positioning pin to mark the corners of the patterns, as shown. Once you have the positioning pin in place,

insert another pin right next to it, taking a very small bite with the pin. The positioning pin will hold the layers of fabric together while you insert the second pin to hold the layers together for sewing. Sew the triangles into rows, then sew all the rows together. Join the rows with a positioning pin to hold the fabric while you pin the sections together.

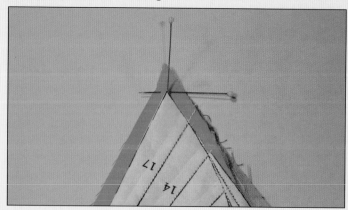

Positioning pin

Adding Pieced Borders

You can use a variety of colors from the center of your quilt to make a pieced border for the edge treatment. For interest, change the width of the strips or the amount of each color used. You can also use the leftover strips used for sewing the blocks.

For 2" finished borders, cut four strips 2½" x 20" of each color. Arrange the strips in the order you want to sew the colors, ranging from very light to very dark in each color family. Sew the strips together with a ¼" seam allowance.

Make cuts across the pieced strips, spacing the cuts 2½" apart (the finished width of 2" plus ½" for seam allowances). Join the cut strips as needed to make your border lengths.

Outside border: Add a 4" (finished) outer border to provide a finishing frame around your beautiful center of windmills.

Finishing: Layer the quilt top, batting, and backing and quilt the layers. Quilt by outlining the shape of the blocks in each windmill. You can add more dimension by stitching just inside the colored sections of the windmills. Remember to quilt in the background section so you will have approximately the same amount of quilting over the surface of the whole quilt. Use your favorite method to bind the raw edges using the same color as the outer border.

Plan your color placement
using this block layout.

The center of each full
windmill is marked with a circle.

Borders & Finishing Touches 2 – Bonnie K. Browning

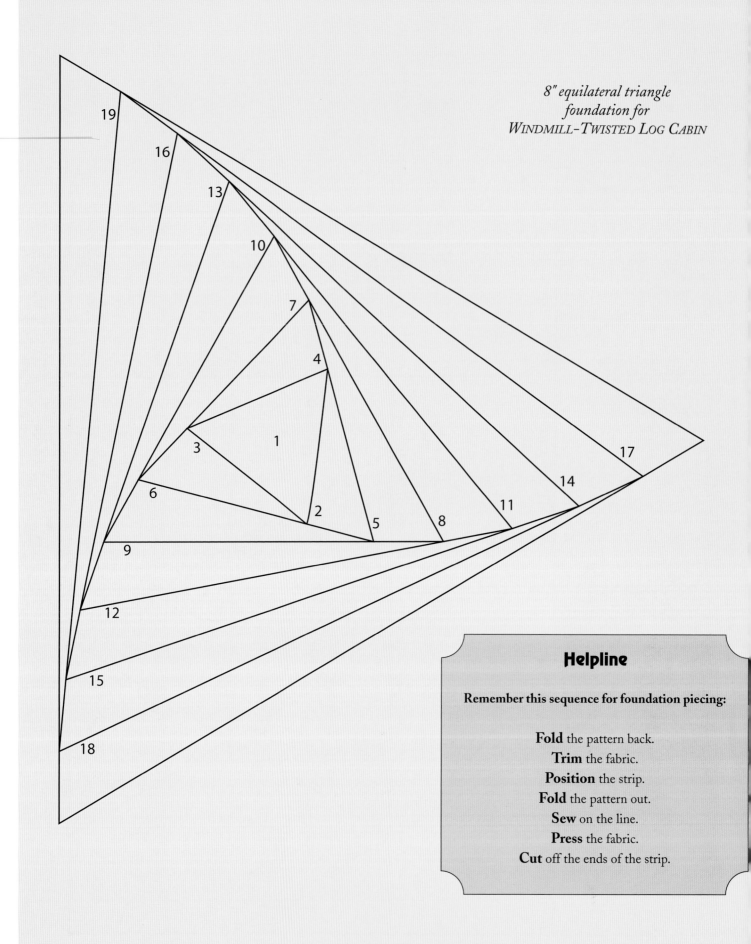

*8" equilateral triangle
foundation for
WINDMILL–TWISTED LOG CABIN*

Helpline

Remember this sequence for foundation piecing:

Fold the pattern back.
Trim the fabric.
Position the strip.
Fold the pattern out.
Sew on the line.
Press the fabric.
Cut off the ends of the strip.

Whig Rose

Appliquéd Border

By Lois Embree Arnold, Montgomery, Alabama. Quilt size: 36" x 36". Finished border: 6" wide.

Technique: Appliquéd undulating vine border

A traditional whig rose appliquéd block is set off by a flowing undulating vine border. The flower design in the center is reduced in scale and set into each corner of the quilt.

Making the Pattern

Trace the center line of the vine (pattern on pages 75–76) onto template plastic and cut out the shape. Place the template over the border fabric and mark the line on the fabric with a very sharp pencil or mechanical pencil.

Cut 150" of 1" wide bias strip for the vine. Fold the strip in half lengthwise, wrong sides together, and press. Open up the strip and press both raw edges into the center, using the center fold as a guide. Press the strip to remove the center crease. Center the bias strip over the line on the border and pin in place.

Using your favorite appliqué technique, appliqué the inner curves of the vine first. When you reach an outer curve, slide your needle under the bias to continue stitching the next inner curve.

Once the inner curves of the vine are stitched, you can then slightly stretch the outer edges of the bias to make the vine lie flat to appliqué them in place. You will again slide your needle under the bias, as needed, to stitch the outer edges of the vine.

Leaves, Buds, and Flowers

Appliqué the stems first, then the leaves, buds, and finally the flowers, just like a flower grows.

For needle-turn appliqué, draw the shape on the right side of the fabric. Cut around the shape ⅛"–¼" outside the drawn line. This allowance is swept under with the side of the needle, one or two stitch lengths ahead of the stitching. Make sure the pencil line is swept under where it won't be seen. Stitches should be close together, approximately ¹⁄₁₆"–⅛" apart with a one- or two-thread bite into the fold of the appliqué. The thread used should be fine and in a color that matches or blends with the fabric being applied to the background.

Place the leaves as shown or feel free to move them around. Just as in nature, no two are exactly alike.

This design is scaled for a 36" quilt. You can make the border longer by adding more of the S curves, keeping the corner and center buds intact.

Quilting

Add some quilting stitches to the leaves and on the surface of the flowers. This will help secure the appliqué to the background and add texture as well. Stipple quilting behind the appliqué makes the vine more prominent.

About Lois Embree Arnold

Lois grew up with quilts made by her mother. A quiltmaker since 1976, Lois enjoys both piecing and appliqué. Her technical proficiency has earned her the title of Princess of Piecing by her closest friends. She has shared her quilts in exhibits at guilds, national quilt shows, and art exhibits, and she teaches across the U.S. and internationally. Lois was one of seven members of the Dubuque Busy Quilters, which had a challenge in the early 1980s and published the experience in American Quilter *magazine, setting off the explosion of challenges among groups all over the country.*

Having recently moved to Alabama with her husband, Gary, Lois is stretching her horizons by combining a variety of art techniques into her quilts. Lois is the author of Pine Tree Quilts, *published by AQS (2000).*

Undulating vine appliqué pattern for 6" wide border

Undulating vine appliqué corner pattern

Keeping Autumn with Me
Floral Appliquéd Border

By Gladi Porsche, Lee, New Hampshire. Quilt size: 93" x 93". Appliquéd floral border with corner block. Border 9" wide.

Technique: Needle-turn Appliqué

This original design is based on the traditional Mariner's Compass block and the Oak Leaf and Real block. The fabric choices were inspired by the gorgeous autumn colors of New England. More than three years in the making, this quilt includes more than 700 needle-turn appliquéd circles and 400 leaves.

Making the pattern

One repeat of the border pattern is provided on pages 80–82. Trace the pattern on template plastic then use the plastic template to create a vellum tracing for the whole border. (Turn the plastic over to trace the mirror-image portions of the undulating vine.) See illustration below. Some sections of the pattern will be mirrored (flip right to left) and rotated 180°.

Leaves, Vines, and Berries

Choose fabrics to represent autumn colors, from bright to dark greens for the leaves, bright to dark red prints for the flowers and berries, and a mottled golden yellow for the background. Look for a dark fabric with bits of color in it to use for the vines. See how the directional print creates a striped effect when cut on the bias. the variation in colors adding texture to the vines.

The main bias vine is a scant ⅜" wide (cut 1⅛"). The smaller bias stems are ¼" wide (cut ¾"). Fold the strips in thirds lengthwise, and baste the vines to the background following the size shown on the pattern.

The berries are ½" in diameter, and the larger circles are ¾" in diameter. Use sticky dots from the office supply store as the patterns for all of the circles.

Quilting

Diagonal quilting lines are stitched in the borders. A more elaborate design would not be needed with the mottled background. The diagonal lines secure the background and show off the appliqué.

About Gladi Porsche

Gladi is a busy physician as the medical director of the University of New Hampshire Student Health Services. In this position, she sees patients, performs administrative duties, and supervises a clinical staff of 24 people. Quilting is her way of relaxing and getting away from the stresses of her work.

Pattern on pages 80–82   *Mirrored pattern*   *Rotate 180°*

Appliqué corner pattern

Section A
Appliqué pattern
9" wide border

Borders & Finishing Touches 2 – Bonnie K. Browning

Section B
Appliqué pattern
9" wide border

C

B

A

Section C
Appliqué pattern
9" wide border

Spice of Life
Peek-A-Boo Borders

By Linda M. Roy, Farragut, Tennessee. Quilt size 82" x 82". Border size: 1½" wide.

Technique: Peek-a-boo appliqué

Peek-a-boo appliqué (named by the author) is made from a combination of straight-of-grain and bias strips. They are used to create a border whose bottom layer peeks through after the edges are rolled back and appliquéd in place.

Prepare the Strips

For a 1½" finished border, make one continuous background strip on the straight of grain 2" wide by the length needed. This is the bottom layer. Also make two bias strips, each cut 2" wide by the length needed for the top layer. Make sure you use true bias. The two bias strips can be cut from the same fabric, or you can use two different fabrics.

Fold each bias strip in half along its length, wrong sides together, and press. Place the bias strips on top of the straight-of-grain strip so that their folded edges meet in the middle. Stitch a scant ¹⁄₁₆" from both raw edges to stabilize the strips.

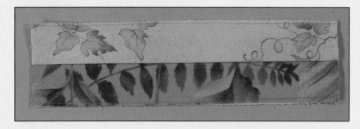

Mark a small dot every 2" on the center folds. Tack stitch, with matching thread, at each dot.

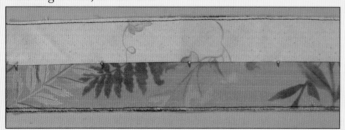

Beginning on one end, roll the bias folded edge back. Hand appliqué the folded edge, starting at the first tack stitch, pivoting slightly at each tack stitch along the entire length of the strip. Turn back the folded edge on the opposite side and appliqué to the end of the strip.

These strips can be inserted as sashing between blocks or used as borders. You can hand quilt in the peek-a-boo single layer of fabric. If you prefer to machine quilt, consider quilting along the folded edges to accentuate the shapes.

Quilting

Show off the shapes by quilting along the turned-back sections of the strip.

As another variation, you can add a decorative stitch on the bottom strip before you cut it into sections for the border.

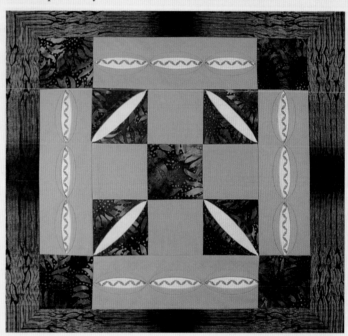

The strips can be cut any width. If the length of your quilt edge is not divisible by 2, use the Making Borders Fit instructions on page 5 to divide the edge of the quilt into equal segments for the tack marks.

About Linda M. Roy

An avid quiltmaker, Linda enjoys designing her own quilts, and she especially loves the versatility of appliqué. She started quilting while living in Arkansas, where she met several quilting friends who shared her interests. She entered her first quilt contest in Little Rock in 1990. Her quilt VICTORIANNA was awarded a first-place ribbon. A major turning point was recognition in the 1993 AQS show with CUPID'S HEART, which won a second place in amateur appliqué. Since winning that first ribbon, Linda has entered many contests and won many awards, including the Hancock's of Paducah Best of Show award at the American Quilter's Society Show in 2004, with her quilt SPICE OF LIFE.

My Turkish Garden
Bound Scalloped Border

By Helen Umstead, Hawley, Pennsylvania. Quilt size: 90" x 90". Bound scallops (appliquéd and faced), 3" base on the arc.

Technique: Bound Scallops (appliquéd and faced)

In MY TURKISH GARDEN, Helen used bound scallops surrounding the central motif and as a finish to the quilt edge. The scallops are made by alternating colors, and the edges of the scallops are covered with narrow bias strips.

Make the Scallops

To divide the edge to be filled with scallops into equal sections, see Making Borders Fit on page 5. For a circular design like the center of TURKISH GARDEN, cut a paper circle the finished size needed for your design. Fold the circle in half and crease the paper. Unfold the paper and match the creased lines to crease the circle again in the other direction.

Continue folding the paper in quarters, eighths, etc. until you reach the size of the base of the scallop that looks pleasing for your quilt. Helen used a 3-inch diameter circle to make her scallops.

You will need ¼" wide bias tape. Make your own with ¾" wide bias strips and a bias-tape maker, or purchase premade bias tape.

Make a 3" diameter circle, or a size that will fit the edge of your quilt. Lay the circle along the edge of the quilt to determine the depth you desire. Usually half a circle will make a good scalloped edge, but the scallop could be more, shallow too.

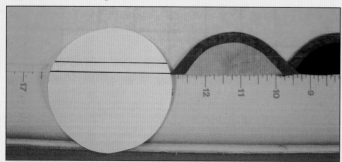

Apply scallops to a background. Cut out the scallops and baste them to the quilt edge with the wrong side of the base of each scallop aligned with the right side of the border edge. Pin in place. Cut bias strips ¾" wide. Appliqué ¼" wide single-fold bias tape over the arc of the scallops, trimming the bias even with the raw edge. Continue until the edges of all of the scallops are covered.

This method works if you are appliquéing the scallops to a background, but for the edge of a quilt, you need to provide a finished backing to the scallops.

Apply scallops to a quilt edge. Your quilting should stop about 1" from the edge to allow you room to work with the scallops. Make sure the edges of your quilt top are straight before adding

the scallops. Trim the edges if necessary and trim the batting ¼" in from the edge of the quilt top and backing of the quilt.

You will prepare individual scallops to apply to the edge of the quilt. Cut two layers of scallops. Place the layers wrong sides together and use a glue stick or fabric spray to hold the two scallops together. If you need extra stability for the scallops on the edge, add a layer of stabilizer or lightweight batting between the two layers of fabric. Cut 1" wide bias strips and fold the raw edges to the center. Bind the edges of each scallop with ¼" bias tape by wrapping the tape from front to back to encase the raw edges.

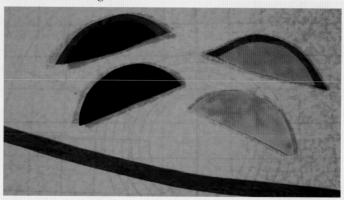

Make all the scallops for the edge and pin them to the backing of the quilt, overlapping them slightly to provide a row of continuous scallops. Make sure the backs of the scallops are next to the backing. Using a ¼" seam allowance, stitch the scallops to the backing *only*. Turn the scallops so they face out from the edge and press.

Appliqué another ¼" bias strip to cover the top edge of the quilt top and the base of the scallops. This bias strip is stitched on the top of the quilt and gives a neat edge to the scallops. If needed, trim the quilt top to reduce any bulk. Stitch both sides of the bias strip. Now your quilt is finished with a beautiful scalloped edge.

About Helen Umstead

Helen Umstead has been quilting since 1995, after making her first quilt as a gift to her first grandchild. Glue-stick appliqué is her favorite technique. She has exhibited her quilts in many shows, including the AQS shows in Paducah, Kentucky, and Nashville, Tennessee. Helen is an active member of the Milford Valley Quilt Guild, Milford, Pennylvania.

94 Yards of Lace

Multiple Shark's Teeth Borders

By Susan Stewart, Pittsburg, Kansas. Quilt size: 76" x 76. Shark's teeth border. Border size: 2".

Technique: Shark's Teeth
Supplies

Fabric: Choose a lightweight, natural fiber. Swiss cotton batiste layered over a subtle quilting cotton print was used in 94 YARDS OF LACE. Most quilting cottons will work as long as they are not loosely woven. Avoid large prints. The three-dimensional texture of the shark's teeth will be lost in a busy print. Use solids or subtle tone-on-tone prints. Prewash, starch, and press the fabric.

Wash-out marker

Rotary-cutting ruler 6" x 24"

Small, sharp, pointed scissors that cut cleanly all the way to the tip

Lightweight thread, such as 80 wt. cotton for batiste, or 60 wt. cotton for quilting cotton fabric (Mettler 60 wt. works well and comes in many colors.)

Sewing machine needles for extra-fine 80 wt. thread and bastiste. Use a size 70 needle. For 60 wt. thread, use a 75 or 80 needle.

Water-soluble glue is helpful. Glue Pins® by Sullivans is Susan's favorite, or Elmer's® Blue Gel School Glue also works, as do glue sticks.

Making Multiple Rows

The directions given here are for three rows of teeth, as shown on the quilt, with a secondary pattern resulting from unstitched portions of the tucks. The tucks are ½" deep, and the teeth are 1" wide. The finished border is 1⅞" wide (2⅜" including seam allowances). For the inner Shark's Teeth border on the quilt, the length of the inner finished edge of the border is 35½", and the length of the outer finished edge of the border is 38⅜".

For the pattern to miter correctly at the corners, the length of the inner finished edges of the border strips must be multiples of 3" minus ½", for example, 35½", 38½", 41½", etc. If your border is a different measurement, consider adding a narrow plain border to reach the required length.

Cut four cross-grain strips of fabric 6" x 42". If your fabric is not 42" wide, piece strips together with a ¼" seam, and press seam allowances open. With a wash-out marker that shows up well on your fabric, draw a line the length of the strips 1½" from one long cut edge. Draw another line the length of the strip 1⁹⁄₁₆" from the first line, and draw a third line 1⁹⁄₁₆" from the second. These lines are fold lines for the three tucks. Press a sharp crease exactly on each drawn line.

Set up your sewing machine so you can sew an accurate ½" tuck. Adjust the needle position so it is exactly ½" from one of the marks on the throat plate and run the fold of the fabric on that mark as you stitch. Alternatively, you can use an adjustable seam guide, tape, or a sticky note to make a guide ½" from the needle. Use an 80 wt. thread for batiste or 60 wt. thread for cotton.

Using a stitch length of 2.0, stitch tucks ½" from each fold line. Press all the tucks in the same direction, so that the needle thread is visible on top. Press again from the wrong side, making sure there are no folds of fabric along the stitching lines. The tucks should almost, but not quite, touch. They should not overlap.

On the right side, on the bottom tuck, make a mark with the wash-out pencil 1½" from the selvage edge of the tucked strips. Make marks 1" apart along the length of the strip, until you have 39 marks. On the second tuck, you will be marking halfway between the marks on the first tuck, as follows: Make one mark on the second tuck halfway between the first two marks on the first tuck, and make another mark 1" from that. Then skip the next place. Continue on, marking two and skipping one.

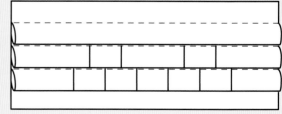

Marks on the upper tuck line up with those on the bottom tuck. They will be halfway between the pairs of marks on the second tuck.

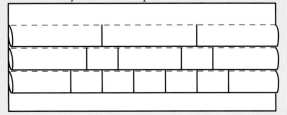

With sharp, pointed scissors that will cut cleanly all the way to the tip, clip the bottom tuck only at the marks. Clip the fabric all the way to, but not through, the stitching line.

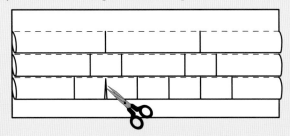

Turn the tucked strip over, and fold the fabric below the clipped tuck back so that you are looking at the underside of the tuck. At each clip, fold the cut edges of the tuck so they lie right along the stitching line. You are forming a V at each clip. Press well. If desired, hold the V shape in place with a tiny bit of water-soluble glue. Press again to dry the glue. (Be sure to test any glue to be certain it washes out after it has been pressed.)

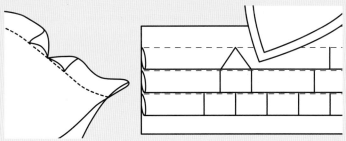

From the right side of the tucked strip, with the fabric below the teeth folded under and out of the way so that you are stitching through the tuck only, stitch a two-step blanket stitch,

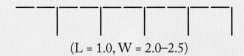

(L = 1.0, W = 2.0–2.5)

or single blanket stitch over the previous stitching.

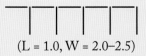

(L = 1.0, W = 2.0–2.5)

Do not use a pin stitch, which has a triple or quintuple straight stitch along with the side-to-side stitch. This type of repetitive stitch builds up too much thread. One swing of the needle should go right into the previous straight stitching. The other swing of the needle should bite into the tuck. Stitch along the full length of the tuck. Press the teeth.

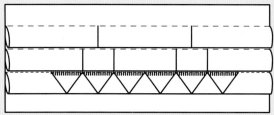

Repeat the steps for the second tuck. When stitching, continue stitching along the unclipped portions of the tuck. Repeat the steps again for the third tuck.

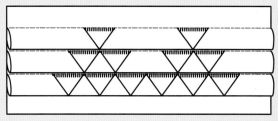

Complete all four shark's teeth border strips. Soak the strips in warm water to remove the glue and markings. Squeeze out the water but do not wring. Roll the fabric tightly in a towel to remove excess water, then press the strips dry from the wrong side.

Trim the border strips: Cut off excess fabric above the shark's teeth, cutting ½" above the stitching line of the third tuck. Cut off the excess fabric below the shark's teeth, cutting ⅜" below points of first row of teeth.

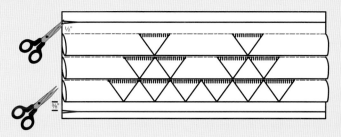

Attaching the Border

The quilt or center medallion to which these borders will be sewn must measure 36" square, which includes ¼" seam allowances.

Fold the quilt and border strips in half and mark their centers. Pin a border strip to the quilt, right sides together, matching the centers. The Vs nearest the ends of the third tuck should line up with the raw edge of the quilt. Begin and end stitching ¼" from the raw edges of the quilt.

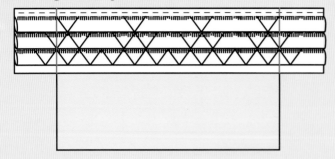

Repeat for all four border strips. Stitching at corners should begin and end at the same point at each corner. Open the border strips and press the seam allowances away from border.

Fold the quilt (right sides together) diagonally at a corner so the borders are lying on top of each other and the point where the border seams meet is at the fold. Pin the borders together so the tuck stitching lines match and the diagonal line formed from the pattern of the shark's teeth on each border strip match. Stitch a diagonal seam through the border, through the points of the Vs, right along the diagonal edge of the teeth.

Back of border

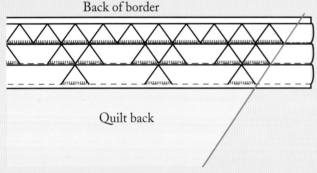

Quilt back

Check the seam from the right side to make sure the tucks aren't caught in the stitching. Trim the mitered seam allowance to ¼" and press the seam allowances open. Repeat for all four corners. Attach additional borders or binding to the shark's teeth border with a ¼" seam allowance.

Making Different Sizes

You can make the shark's teeth in different sizes. Use the following chart for making tucks ½", ¾" or 1" deep. Using the formulas (in parentheses) in the table, you can make tucks in any size you want. Choose the depth of the finished tuck (x) and calculate the distance between fold lines (3x + ¹⁄₁₆"), and the distance between clip marks (2x).

Depth of finished tuck (x)	Distance between fold lines (3x + ¹⁄₁₆")	Distance between clip marks (2x)
½"	1⁹⁄₁₆"	1"
¾"	2⁵⁄₁₆"	1½"
1"	3¹⁄₁₆"	2"

Determining Border Length

The width of the tucks and the number of tucks determine the possible length of the border strips to have corners that miter properly.

The length of the finished edge of the border is a multiple of two times the number of rows times the width of the tucks, minus ½" from the total length. To calculate other lengths, insert the correct number of rows and the width of the tucks into the formula.

Multiple Of Two		Number of Rows		Width of Tucks	Minus ½"		Length of Border Strip
2	x	6	x	1"	− ½"	=	11½"
2	x	8	x	1"	− ½"	=	15½"
2	x	10	x	1"	− ½"	=	19½"
2	x	16	x	1"	− ½"	=	31½"

Variations

You can vary the design by changing the spacing of the clips. Use the graph paper to draw your design before making your clips. See illustrations on page 91-92.

About Susan Stewart

A lover of the fine heirloom sewing techniques for garments, Susan (Pennington) Stewart studied techniques in antique garments and developed her own machine methods for making them. After discovering triangular flaps on an apron, she saw that they were formed by clipping tucks then folding the clipped edges under and stitching. A visit to a museum and the sight of the rows upon rows of overlapping triangular teeth on a huge great white shark looked just like what she was stitching. The name "shark's teeth" was born. Sue has taught this method at Martha Pullen events and has shared the instructions in several publications.

Try multiple rows of shark's teeth to create a center quilt panel or a pillow.
Design is not shown to scale.

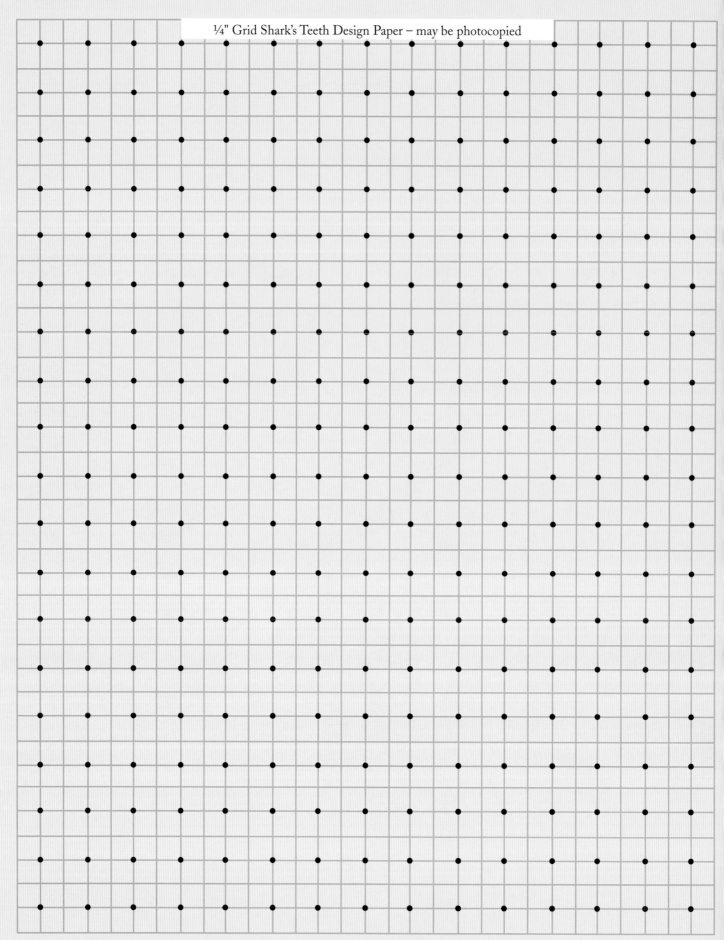

¼" Grid Shark's Teeth Design Paper – may be photocopied

Merdie's Poppies

Shaped Border with Piping

Appliquéd by Lynda Smith and the author. Quilted by Irene Reising. Quilt size: 39" x 39". Collection of Meredith & Bill Schroeder. Center design is a variation of the Clump of Poppies pattern by Susan R. DuLaney, www.DistinctivePieces.com.

Technique: Shaped Border with Piping

You can add pizzazz to the edge of your quilt by adding shaped borders with piping. The little bit of extra color in the piping gives you an opportunity to bring a color from the center of the quilt to the edge. The shape can be an undulating vine, or it can be zigzag lines.

Example: Begin by appliquéing a design in the center of a 40" square of fabric. Leave the outer 6" on all edges plain, without any appliqué. This is the space you will use for adding the piped border.

Cut four 6" x 40" fabric strips for the borders and cut four 6" x 40" pieces of freezer paper.

Freezer Paper Pattern

Mark off a 6" square at each end of a freezer-paper strip. These squares will be the corners of the border and will be mitered to create the sharp points where the borders come together. Fold the freezer paper on the marked lines.

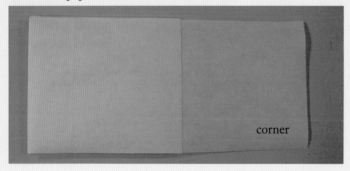

corner

Match the folds at each end and make a crease in the center of the freezer paper. This will give you two equal sections along the edge of the quilt. You need four sections, so fold each section one more time. (Remember to fold accordion-style.) Now, there are four equal sections and the two corner squares. Draw an undulating vine shape on the one of the four equal sections. The shape on the corners can be the same as the other segments, or you can cut the angle sharper as shown in MERDIE'S POPPIES.

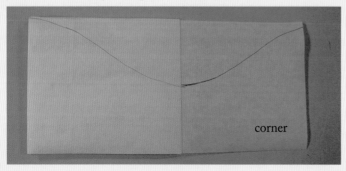

corner

Fold and cut the shape on the drawn vine for each of the four freezer-paper strips.

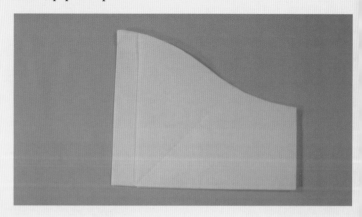

Iron the freezer paper on the fabric border strips. Using a fabric marker, mark the fabric along the undulating paper shape. Do not cut the fabric yet.

Prepare four strips of piping at least 40" long. See pages 24–25 for instructions on making the piping. Cut the bias strips 1½" wide and sew a ¼" cording into the center. Place a zipper foot or a cording foot on your sewing machine. Stitch the piping to the fabric border, placing the raw edge of the piping along the drawn undulating line.

Trim away the excess fabric, leaving ¼" seam allowance from the stitched line. (Use regular scissors and eyeball the seam allowance.) Press the seam allowances under the piped edge.

Attaching the Border

Pin the borders in place, one at a time, matching the straight edge of the border to the raw edge of the quilt center. Mark 45-degree angles in each corner with a fabric marker. Place an edge-stitching foot on the sewing machine and start stitching about 1" from the angled corner mark. Take a couple of stitches to make sure the needle falls between the piping and the border fabric. Adjust the needle position as necessary. Stitch in the ditch along the piping with thread that matches the piping.

Appliquéing the miters allows you to fold under the border where it meets in the corners. This gives you flexibility to make the mitered corner just meet or you can angle the miter to make a deeper V in the corner.

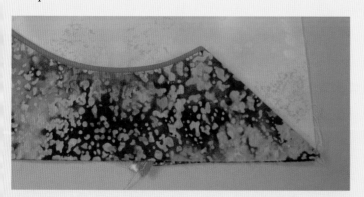

After all four borders are stitched in place, appliqué the miters in the corners.

Trim away the center fabric under the border to reduce the bulk.

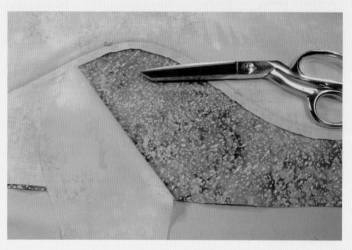

Now you are ready to quilt and finish your quilt.

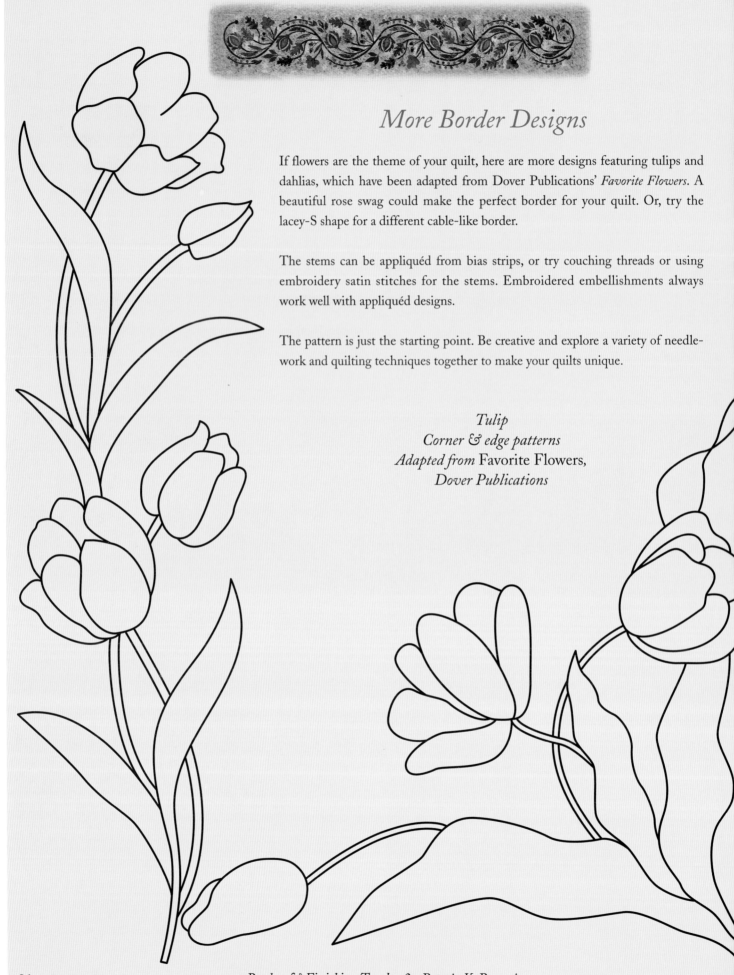

More Border Designs

If flowers are the theme of your quilt, here are more designs featuring tulips and dahlias, which have been adapted from Dover Publications' *Favorite Flowers*. A beautiful rose swag could make the perfect border for your quilt. Or, try the lacey-S shape for a different cable-like border.

The stems can be appliquéd from bias strips, or try couching threads or using embroidery satin stitches for the stems. Embroidered embellishments always work well with appliquéd designs.

The pattern is just the starting point. Be creative and explore a variety of needle-work and quilting techniques together to make your quilts unique.

Tulip
Corner & edge patterns
Adapted from Favorite Flowers,
Dover Publications

Dahlia
Corner & edge patterns
Adapted from Favorite Flowers,
Dover Publications

Posy Ribbon Swag

*Posy Ribbon Swag pattern
for 8½" wide border*

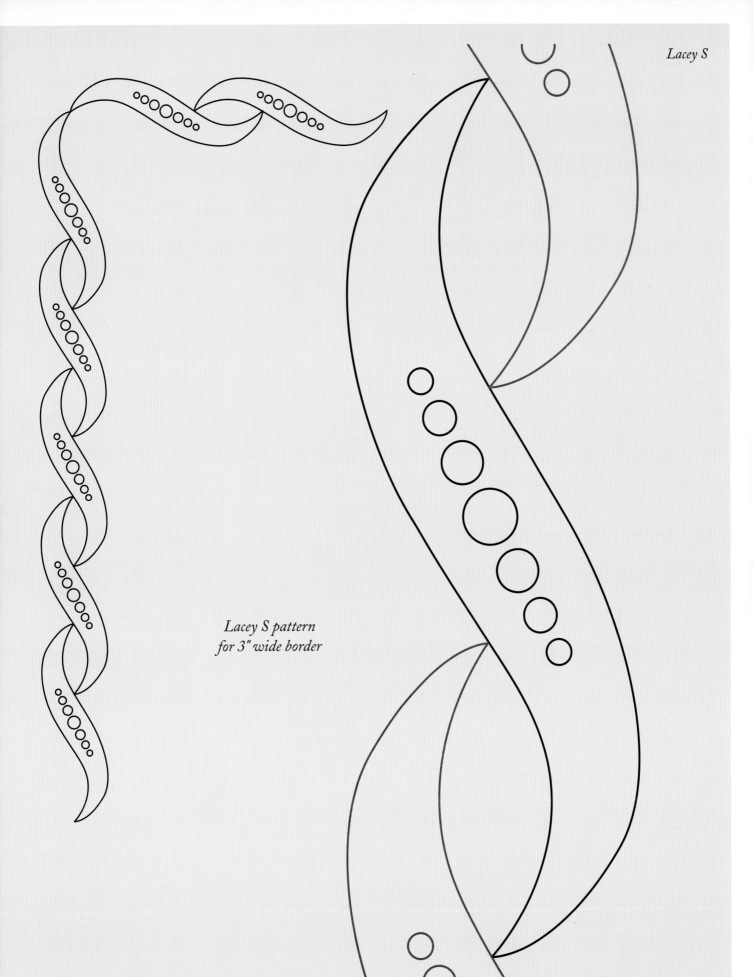

*Lacey S pattern
for 3" wide border*

Faux Feathers

Faux Feathers

Faux Feathers
Border pattern
for 4" wide border

*Aussie Leaves pattern
for 3½" wide border
Adapted from a mosaic
floor, Melbourne, Australia*

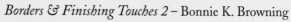

*Aussie Leaves
corner pattern*

Ivy Vine pattern for 3½" border
Adapted from Favorite Flowers,
Dover Publications

Ivy Vine
corner pattern

*Regal Rose pattern
for 5" wide border*

Borders Are Not Just for Quilts

Borders designed for quilts can easily be adapted for other projects. Try the Peek-A-Boo technique on page 84, or the split half-square border to decorate the top edges of sheets and pillowcases. Use some of the decorative stitches on your sewing machine to stitch the edges of the borders to the sheets.

Sheet & pillowcase with split half-square border

Split Half-square Border for Sheets & Pillowcases

The split half-square is a unit that can be sewn together in a variety of ways. It can look like a ribbon running around the edges of your quilt, or play with the placement of the triangles for other looks.

Begin planning your border by determining how many blocks are required to fit the edges of your quilts. See Making Borders Fit on page 5. Fold the paper and measure from fold to fold to determine the size of pieced blocks you need for your quilt. To the finished size of your block, you will add 1¼" to your measurement for the light and dark fabrics; and add ⅞" to your measurement for the medium fabric.

Sewing a 3" Finished Ribbon Border: To make a 3" wide finished ribbon border, cut a 4¼" strip each of light and dark fabrics; recut into 4¼" squares. One 4¼" strip will make approximately 10 squares, depending on the width of your fabric.

Draw a diagonal line from corner to corner. Place the squares right sides together and stitch ¼" on both sides of the drawn line. Cut apart on the drawn line.

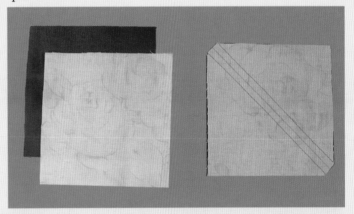

Cut a 3⅞" strip of medium-value fabric; recut into squares. Draw a diagonal line from corner to corner. Place the square, right sides together, with one of the light/dark half-squares. The drawn line of the square should be aligned with the plain (not sewn) corners of the light/dark square.

Stitch ¼" on both sides of the drawn line. Cut on the drawn line. You will have two split half-squares that are mirror images. For some layouts, you can use this to your advantage to reverse the design at the center of the border edge.

Play with this pieced unit to create the borders for the sheet and pillowcases. Press the seams open for a smoother finish.

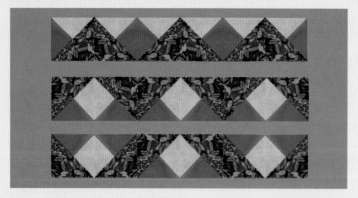

Sewing the Border

Stitch split half-squares together to fit the width of the sheet or pillowcases. Cut a strip of stabilizer (like Sew'N Wash) the same size as the assembled border, which will dissolve when the sheet is washed. Place the stabilizer on the right side of the border and sew along both long edges with a ¼" seam allowance. Leave the ends free for turning.

Turn the strip right side out and press. Measure the width of the hem on the top of the sheet. Subtract the finished width of the border and divide that measurement by two to determine the placement of the border from the top edge of the sheet.

Draw a placement line along the edge of the sheet. With pins, mark the center of the border and the sheet. Starting from the center, pin the top and bottom edges of the border to the sheet.

Sew the border to the sheet using a straight stitch close to the edge, or choose a decorative stitch. To finish the ends of the border, turn under the excess fabric and topstitch. Use the same technique to sew borders to the pillowcases.

Pillow with Peek-A-Boo Appliquéd Border

Using fabrics from the border on the sheet, make a pillowcase with a decorative sleeve to fit a 12" x 16" pillow form. See page 84 for the Peek-A-Boo Appliqué technique.

Making the Pillowcase

Cut a 12" x 16" rectangle for the top of the pillowcase. For the back, cut two 12" x 19½" rectangles of fabric. Fold each back piece in half with wrong sides together. To assemble the pillowcase, lay the two back pieces, right sides together, with the top, aligning the raw edges. The back pieces will overlap 3" in the center. This makes it easy to change or launder the pillow cover.

For a couture look to your pillow—no pointy corners—use the corner template shown below to taper the corners. Mark the corners and trim. Sew the pillowcase together, using ¼" seam allowances. Turn the pillowcase right side out and insert the pillow form. You have just completed a pillowcase with NO zippers and NO pointy corners.

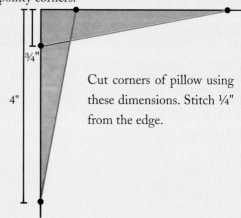

¾"

4"

Cut corners of pillow using these dimensions. Stitch ¼" from the edge.

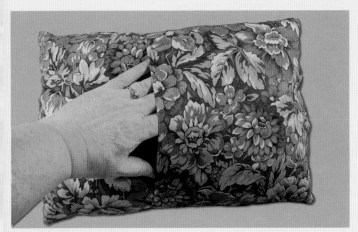

Decorative Sleeve

A removable sleeve with a decorative border slides over the pillowcase. Cut three light-colored background strips 3" x 24½", to fit around the pillow. Using a washout marker, draw a line down the center of each strip. Stitch a decorative design down the center of each strip. This can be the same design or use a variety of stitches on your sewing machine. If you use a directional stitch (one that moves the needle in multiple directions) guide the fabric so it stays parallel with the edge of the foot on the machine.

Cut four *bias* strips 3" x 24½" in a color that contrasts with the pillow and the light-colored strips. Fold the strips in half lengthwise with wrong sides together. Baste two strips to two of the light strips, matching raw edges. The folded edges should meet in the center.

Mark the strips in equal sections and tack the folds. It's time to fold the edges to create the Peek-A-Boo effect. Pin the bias strips to the background periodically to keep the fabric from moving as you stitch the folded edges. Use a featherstitch to sew

the folded bias edges in place and you can stitch a continuous line by alternating from one side to the other.

Sew the remaining light strip in the center of a piece of batting 12" x 26" by stitching a scant ¼" from both long edges. Sew a Peek-A-Boo appliquéd strip to each side of the center strip, using ¼" seam allowances. Press the band. Add any quilting stitches now. Trim away the excess batting.

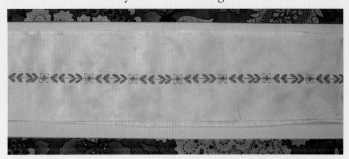

Cut a facing rectangle the same size as the band. Place the facing fabric, right sides together, with the band and sew along the long edges using a ¼" seam allowance. Turn the band right side out and press. Pin the right sides of the ends of the top and batting together. Using a ¼" seam allowance, stitch the top and batting together so the band makes a circle.

Turn under and blindstitch the ends of the facing to complete the band. Slide the band over the pillow. Your pillow with the Peek-A-Boo appliquéd band is finished. For a change of season, make bands in lighter colors for summer and darker colors for winter.

Lesson Plan for Instructors

Notes to Instructors and Shop Owners:

Making borders with pizazz is easy when they are approached with confidence. *Borders & Finishing Touches 2* provides the instructions and tips for sewing successful borders and other special touches for today's quiltmakers.

A class on *Borders & Finishing Touches 2* will help you guide students through the various steps to be able to handle borders for their next quilting projects. As a shop owner, you can choose to do in-store demonstrations as a supplement to their purchase of the book, or offer hands-on classes based on projects in the book.

Walk through a variety of techniques to make borders:

Straight butted borders

Multiple straight borders

Mitered borders

Striped borders

Add a special finish to the edge of the quilt:

Binding

Prairie Points (single, two-colored, continuous-strip)

Scalloped edge

Piping (flat, single, multiple, shaped, shells)

Demos and Classes on Borders:

Making the Borders Fit Demo – 30 minutes

Demonstrate how to fold adding-machine tape to make borders that fit.

Mitered Border Demo using step-by-step models – 3 hours

Square up a small quilt.

Review various styles of borders.

Show step-by-step samples of a mitered border.

Have students bring a quilt for discussion on border types that fit the quilt.

Hands-on Border Class – 5 hours

Use small quilts (14" square quilt sandwiches) that will require several fat quarters to use in class.

Measure and square up a quilt; calculate the size of the borders.

Add straight butted borders to one small quilt.

Add mitered borders to one small quilt.

Hands-on Border Class – 3–4 weeks

Choose one of the projects in the book and schedule multi-sessions using the instructions in the book.

Demos and classes on Finishing Touches:

Binding Demo – 30 minutes

Straight corners

Mitered corners

Binding Class – 3 hours

Straight binding corners

Mitered binding corners

Prairie Points (single, two-colored, continuous-strip)

Binding Class – 5 hours

Straight binding corners

Mitered binding corners

Prairie Points (single, two-colored, continuous-strip)

Scalloped edge

Piping (flat, single, multiple, shaped, shells)

About the Author

Since she was a small girl, Bonnie has been making things with her hands. From mud pies to hollyhock dolls, and then on to handicrafts, photography, and sewing, she continues to enjoy the creative process and seeing the finished product.

After making her first quilt in the late 1970s, Bonnie has been an avid quiltmaker. She has been teaching since the mid-1980s and was certified as a quilt judge in 1986. She judges and teaches for quilt guilds and conferences around the world. Her goal is to teach students techniques that they can use in future projects, and to enjoy the process.

Bonnie keeps busy as the executive show director of quilt shows for the American Quilter's Society, and as technical consultant for the AQS *American Quilter* television series. She has appeared on HGTV's *Simply Quilts*, PBS's *Sew Young, Sew Fun*, and the HGTV special, *Quilts, Secrets Hidden in Fabric*. She has authored nine books, published by AQS. If you wonder when she has time to quilt, ask her and she'll tell you that she *makes* time to quilt!

Bonnie resides in Paducah, Kentucky, with her husband, Wayne, and two spoiled cats, White Socks and Tuffy. Check out her Web site at http://bonniebrowning.tripod.com and try putting together the puzzles she creates from her quilts and photos.

Other AQS Books

This is only a small selection of the books available from the American Quilter's Society. AQS books are known worldwide for timely topics, clear writing, beautiful color photos, and accurate illustrations and patterns. The following books are available from your local bookseller, quilt shop, or public library.

#5705   us$22.95

#6805   us$22.95

#6904   us$21.95

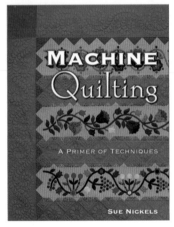

#6299   us$24.95

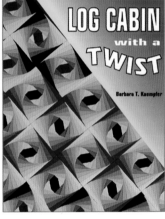
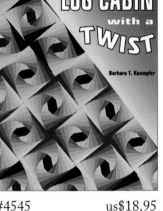

#4545   us$18.95

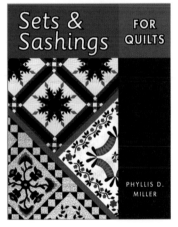

#5590   us$24.95

#6905   us$24.95

#6897   us$22.95

#6799   us$22.95